The Complete Book of
WATER SPORTS

The
Complete Book of

Arthur Liebers

WATER SPORTS

COMPLETELY ILLUSTRATED

Revised Edition

Coward, McCann & Geoghegan, Inc.
New York

Contents

Part II. WATER SPORTS FOR POOL OR BEACH

9. ACTIVITIES FOR THE POOL OR
    WATERFRONT   169

Introduction

SCIENTISTS trace man's long line of ascent from
creatures which lived in the water and came up to dry land
some 300 million years ago. The last few decades have wit-
nessed an unparalleled return of man to water, but this
time for sport and recreation. More leisure time, more
money to spend on recreation, and the adoption of beach
and pool wear which allows untrammeled use of the limbs
and freer exposure to the sun—to say nothing of spectators—
have all aided the burgeoning popularity of water sports.

Swimming has become a part of the life of almost every
American. Its recognition as perhaps the most suitable
form of exercise for persons of all ages and its importance
as a safety factor for participation in any form of water
sport have made us a nation of swimmers. Many schools
today include swimming in the curriculum and some insist
on a certain degree of aquatic proficiency as a requirement
for graduation.

The flourishing home swimming pool industry is a testi-
monial to an increased interest in the water as is the continued demand, and steadily increasing value, of waterfront
property in vacation and residential areas. Technological
development has also spurred the growth in aquatic activity.
The outboard motorboat has brought many millions closer
to the water, and the use of diving and underwater breathing equipment has opened new vistas for thousands of
water sportsmen and women.

11

While the old swimming hole holds a cherished place in the literature of American boyhood, swimming and diving as competitive sports are fairly recent developments dating from the nineteenth century. Rock carvings indicate that the Assyrians crossed small rivers using inflated skins to support them, and the inflated water wings in popular use in the 1920's and 30's served the same purpose for learners and nonswimmers.

Swimming was first recognized as a necessary military skill, and perhaps the first book on the subject *De Arte Natandi* by Everard Digby, published in England in 1587, stressed the value of the skill in approaching an enemy or escaping through the water. Likewise, the ancient samurai of Japan developed a repertoire of swimming techniques for military use.

The Complete Book of Water Sports provides information on all aspects of aquatic sport from games for toddlers in the family pool or at the beach to the techniques of scuba diving. It is hoped that this book will not only be of value to the individual who finds his recreation in the water, but also to the parent and camp or pool director who is looking for ways to channel the energy of his waterborne charges into amusing, interesting and instructive avenues of aquatic activity.

I

MODERN WATER SPORTS

Chapter 1

WATER SKIING

FEW sights in sports are more spectacular than a skier (or skiers) whipping through the water behind a fast boat in wide curves and performing the "aquabatics" that make water skiing so exciting. Actually, however, not many other sports make so few demands on the participant. Toddlers and even those beyond middle age can enjoy water skiing. It is a sport in which most of the work is done by the motor of the pulling boat, and with a life belt only a minimal amount of swimming ability is required. After 10 minutes or so of instruction, the average person with fair muscular co-ordination can set out on water skis and make a presentable showing.

Water-skiing enthusiasts claim that theirs is the fastest growing sport in America today, and it is a fairly safe sport. The few accidents which do occur are generally due to the inexperience or negligence of the driver of the boat. Falling is an expected part of the sport, but falling into the water from a pair of skis may create a big splash without any effects on the skier. At normal skiing speeds, the hazard from a water spill is very slight. However, at speeds of over 30 miles an hour the impact with the water can be unpleasant, and advanced maneuvers such as jumping over ramps introduce an element of hazard.

With the increasing interest in water skiing, most water-front and lake resort areas provide facilities for renting skis and tow boats, and many have schools which provide instruction. Rates may be a bit high. In some places the charge is about $25 an hour, with an instructor skiing alongside the student to advise and aid him.

The Skis

In recent years the tendency has been for shorter water skis. When the sport was first started, in the 20's, the skis were about 10 feet long and flat bottomed. Modern skis— except for special "trick" or "turn-around" skis—have one or 2 fins toward the rear and are seldom much over 6 feet in length.

For comfortable skiing, the foot binding should fit properly. Some skis come with fixed-size binding, others are adjustable, and many water skiers prefer to make their own, using pieces of truck tire or soft rubber. In most adjustable bindings, the unit consists of 2 pieces, with a fixed toe piece and an adjustable heel binding. Some types of permanent bindings consist of the rubber piece or pieces attached to a metal plate which is affixed to the ski. All ski bindings should be made so that they will release readily when the skier falls or wants "out."

While some water skis have been made of fiberglass or fiberglass-covered wood, most water skiers prefer wooden skis, with ash and hickory as first choice, although some are made of mahogany, teak or walnut. Generally the skis are enameled or varnished, and experts claim that the varnish finish gives a faster ride, since it creates less friction than enamel. Like snow skiers, many of the water fraternity wax the bottoms of the skis with paraffin to further eliminate friction drag.

The toes of water skis are pointed upward to prevent the

ski from digging into a wave and performing a toss similar to the "pitchpolling" of a boat.

SKI SELECTION CHART*

(Weight of skier in pounds; minimum ski length required. Experienced skiers may use smaller skis and less horsepower than indicated.)

WEIGHT		75-100	100-125	125-150	150-175	175-200	200-250	2 SKIERS	3 SKIERS
HORSEPOWER	10-15	5½ FT. AND UP	6 FT. AND UP	EXP'D SKIER ONLY	NOT PRACTICAL	NOT PRACTICAL	NOT PRACTICAL	EXP'D SKIERS ONLY	NOT PRACTICAL
	16-20	5 FT. AND UP	5½ FT. AND UP	6 FT. AND UP	EXP'D SKIER ONLY	NOT PRACTICAL	NOT PRACTICAL	EXP'D SKIERS ONLY	NOT PRACTICAL
	21-30	4½ FT. AND UP	5 FT. AND UP	5½ FT AND UP	6 FT. AND UP	6 FT. AND UP	EXP'D SKIERS ONLY	6 FT. AND UP	EXP'D SKIERS ONLY
	31-40	4 FT. AND UP	4½ FT. AND UP	5 FT. AND UP	5½ FT. AND UP	6 FT. AND UP	EXP'D SKIERS ONLY	5½ FT. AND UP	6 FT. AND UP
	OVER 40	4 FT. AND UP	4 FT. AND UP	4½ FT. AND UP	5 FT. AND UP	5½ FT. AND UP	6 FT. AND UP	5 FT. AND UP	5½ FT. AND UP

Courtesy: Evinrude Motors

Among other differences in water skis, some have tapered trailing edges, others run full width. Some experienced skiers prefer the tapered type which they feel gives them better control on fast turns. The better grades of water skis are made of laminated woods which reduce the possibility of cracking or splitting, although most skis will have a tendency to warp after much use and should then be replaced.

The Tow Line

Through trial and error over the years, it has been found that a tow line of 75 feet is best for most water skiing. A shorter line will pull the skier too close to the boat's spray and back wake, and a longer line will probably drag in the water. The 75-foot line is required in competition.

Tow ropes come in a variety of materials, the most popular in recent years being the braided plastics, such as polyethylene and polyroplene, which float and come in different colors. Although double handles are still available, single handles, about a foot long, are now almost universally used. Most of them bought commercially are cushioned for greater comfort.

Flotation devices are recommended for safety and are required in many competitions. They range from simple coated foamed plastic belts to the more expensive—and protective—jackets worn by most of the best competitive skiers.

The Skier's Boat

It is important that a proper combination of boat and motor be used for water skiing. An average, well-performing ski boat is a 14-foot boat with a wide beam, 60 to 70 inches, equipped with a 25- to 40-horsepower motor. This combination is the required minimum to pull one skier with two persons in the boat, the driver and the observer. It is especially important that the ski boat have a wide beam for safety in cornering and stability against the pull of a strong skier cutting sharply to the side of the boat.

For greater versatility, a 15- to 17-foot boat powered by a 50- to 100-horsepower motor will pull two or three skiers with more passengers in the board. Also popular in this size range are the inboard-outboard types, which some users find have less of a wake problem than the more powerful outboards.

Inboard boats also perform well for skiing and are preferred by some. Inboards, 15 to 18 feet long, with 90- to 210-horsepower engines have worked well in pulling skiers. However, it should be kept in mind that in general an inboard requires a larger maneuvering area than an outboard combination.

Tow Hitches

The attachment of the tow line to the boat is most important, especially in outboards, where the rope must be hitched so that on swings and turns it will clear the motor, which is usually the highest point on the stern of the boat. There are a number of different types of tow bars and brackets on the market. The rope should be attached to the boat fairly high, so that there will be less chance of its fouling the propeller when it is dropped by the skier. Also, for any trick skiing, the rope should be high enough to keep it from dragging in the water when a bit of slack develops in the line.

Many outboards are equipped with 2 lifting handles on the transom, but there are several reasons why they should not be used to hold the ski line. They are usually too low and are seldom strong enough to stand the steady strain of pulling a skier. Likewise, mooring cleats on the stern deck are not too satisfactory for this purpose. Some types of tow bars attach to the transom, pass around outside the motor, and have a pulley follower that rides around the bar, but they should be arranged to allow sufficient room for the motor to tilt if it strikes an underwater obstruction. The preferred types are those which carry the line over the top of the motor. With inboards, perhaps the best arrangement is a pylon or post, bolted to the beams of the boat, set on the centerline somewhere between the middle of the boat and the transom; and it should be at least 3 feet high. With this type of hitch, care should be taken to remove any stern fittings, cleats, or other fixtures which could snag the line. As to windshields, some operators keep them on; others prefer to remove them when pulling skiers, since they may become covered with spray, which reduces visibility. Another helpful accessory for water-ski pulling is a boarding ladder, or thick, knotted rope to facilitate getting aboard.

In most inboards, the standard propeller will serve well for towing skiers. For most outboards, lower-pitch propellers specially designed for towing skiers are available, although these should not be used at full throttle when not pulling skiers—to avoid overspeeding the engine with the possibility of permanent injury to the motor.

How to Water Ski

The first step toward learning to water ski is taken on dry land. Using properly fitted skis of the right length, place them side by side on a level stretch of beach or grass. First, wet your feet and the bindings, then push your foot up comfortably snug in the binding and pull up the heel piece. Then sit on your skis and stretch your arms straight out, knees between your elbows. Take a firm hold on the handle of the tow rope, and have someone pull you up to a standing position. Do not try to do any pulling yourself; the boat will do all the pulling in the water. The important points to keep in mind are: arms straight; knees bent; leave the pulling to the boat.

Many beginners find that the most comfortable way to hold the tow handle is in an overhand grip with the palms facing down. Try to hold the bar with the fingers rather than with the entire hand, as a hand hold is liable to cause blisters across the palms.

The proper skiing position is this: body in a crouch; tips of skis above water; arms straight ahead; back straight; and knees bent. Things to avoid are leaning forward, straightening the knees, and uneven distribution of weight on the skis.

Selecting the water ski. Perhaps the most important feature is a binding that holds the foot comfortably.

Both the foot and the binding should be wet
when the ski is fitted to the foot.

Any of these may cause you to fall off balance the moment the pull of the boat on the line reaches you.

It may help the first few times to have someone hold the tips of the skis up in proper position.

The Take-Off

The best start for the beginner is the deep-water start, which means in water that is 3 feet or more deep. The operator will bring the boat around and drag the rope near you so that you can get the handle and grip it. Get in the skiing position, knees high, almost against your chest. When you are set and ready, call "Gear" to the boat. That is the operator's signal to move slowly ahead at idling speed until the slack is out of the rope. When you feel tension in the rope, shout "Hit it!" and the boat will accelerate rapidly, pulling you up on the water. Do not pull back on the rope. As you feel the pull grow stronger, stand up slowly, keeping your weight on your heels, not leaning forward or backward. Try to keep your skis parallel and about 18 inches apart. If your ski tips head for each other or spread apart, it is a sign that your ankles are turned. If you keep your knees about 18 inches apart and your feet pointed ahead, the skis will behave!

There are two sensations you must get used to on water skis. You will feel your skis wobble and think you are going to fall, but a little fight to keep your balance will probably correct this wobbling. Hold onto the handle of the tow until you are sure you are really going over. A little shift in weight will usually keep you on top of your skis. The other new sensation comes when you feel a bit of slack in the line. The natural reaction is to pull back on the handle, which will result in pulling you forward. Then, when the boat picks up the slack and the line tautens, you will be pulled off balance and go over. If you relax for a moment and give the boat a chance, the slack will be taken up and you will again have the support of the line.

In a shallow water take-off, you sit on the trailing ends of your skis, with knees bent. As the boat speeds up, get into proper skiing position with knees bent.

In many places the start is from a dock. Knowing how to take off from a dock is therefore important, and not too difficult. Also the dock start is good to know, as it is a means of "dry" water skiing with no need to get more than your toes wet—unless you take a fall. Sit at the edge of the dock, facing the transom of the boat with the tips of your skis out of water and your knees raised slightly from the dock. Place 7 or 8 feet of the line on the dock near you where you can watch it, and where it can run out without catching on anything. Or you may find it easier to hold the coiled rope in your hand.

Hold the tow handle. When you are heady to go, call out "Gear." As the boat starts, watch the portion of rope you have placed on the dock, and as it plays out, call "Hit it!" and transfer your weight to the skis. At this point avoid leaning back or your skis may slip out from under you, and do not lean forward or you may be pitched ahead into the water. The crouch should be fairly deep and the handle should be held low to give you better balance at the start. It may take a few attempts to develop the right timing for this start. Wait for the boat to pull you. Do not jump off too soon.

Turning

For your first few minutes on water skis, stay well within the wake of the boat that is pulling you. If you move outside the wake, the waves will probably throw you. An experienced operator can help your first runs by having his boat follow your course instead of making you follow his.

If you have ever done any snow skiing it will make the

A "dry run" precedes the first lesson. Note the preferable overhand grip on the ski tow handle, with both palms facing downward.

Ready for take-off. The skis are kept together; the skier sits on trailing edge of skis with knees bent, waiting for the boat to start.

technique of turning on water skis much easier to acquire. When you want to turn on water skis, you must bank by raising the edges of the skis as well as pointing them where you want to go. Say you want to go to the right. Lean over to the right—at your ankles—and at the same time raise the left edges of the skis higher than the right. The skis will turn to the right. You will find that the skis are more responsive to a bank at low speeds than at high. The faster you are going, the deeper you must dig with the edge of the skis to make your turn, and you must crouch lower to keep your balance. Until you have gained some confidence in turning from side to side, stay within the wake of the boat.

Reaching Calm Water

One of the greatest thrills of water skiing is crossing the wake of the boat for the first time and skiing in the calm water beyond it. The basic principle in crossing the wake is to approach the turbulent water as close to a 90-degree angle as possible. In this way you avoid having your skis caught in the trough of the wake. To get set for the "crossing," slide over to the opposite side of the wake you are riding, then reverse your turn, head for the wake, and ride through it. Here, to hesitate is to be lost. Once you start through the wake, keep on moving through it. If you slow down in the midst of the turbulent water you will very probably lose your skis. It might help if you tried to cross your wake when the boat is turning. There is a slightly flatter wake at such times, and you can get some additional speed across it by swinging away from the direction in which the boat is turning.

After you have crossed the wake a few times, you will probably want to try your hands—or feet—at jumping it. This is not too difficult. Approach the wake at nearly right angles—from the outside is easier. Spring upwards just as the tips touch the wake; absorb the shock of landing with your

As the boat starts off, the skier rises out of the water, gradually straightens knees and rises as the skis reach planing speed.

knees. Remember to keep your back as straight as possible on the jump, and keep your toes up. With some practice you should be able to jump a wake with about 3 feet of air under your skis.

Falling and Recovery

If you water ski, there are times when you will fall. At low speeds—around 20 miles an hour—it does not matter much how you hit the water. But at higher speeds you should know how to hit the water safely. The safest way to hit the water at 35 miles an hour or faster is with a somersault or roll. After you have dropped the tow-line handle, fold your arms in front of your face, tuck your head behind your arms for protection, and roll up into a ball before hitting the water. With proper practice this way of falling will become almost automatic. Also, try to fall to the side of the skis to avoid hitting them during the fall or when you come up for air.

The next problem is to recover the skis and get them on again. The first few times you may find yourself engaged in a mad scramble with two skis that won't stay where you want them. There is a simple way to manage this: get the skis close to you, parallel to each other, and facing in the proper direction. Pull your knees up against your chest, and take a deep breath. Duck under water, face forward, and slip one foot into the binding. Reach out for the other ski, and repeat. You will find that you will sink only a few inches under water, and if you are wearing a life belt, you do not even have to duck your head under water to get the skis on. Go out in water that is shoulder deep a few times and practice putting on your skis so that you will know how. Then you won't have to put up with the caustic comments of a boat operator who is circling around waiting for you to get set.

There are times when you will want to get out of your

skis. You do not have to reach under water to free your foot. Merely bend your knee, kick straight down, and then pull your knee up again, fast. This will almost always pull your feet out of the bindings, if done quickly enough, and the ski will float to the surface.

The Landing

Landing is just about the least of the problems in water skiing. Release the tow rope and you will sink into the water. Use the technique explained above to free the skis and carry them into shore. However, most skiers who end a run erect prefer a more spectacular finish. If there is a landing ramp or gently sloping beach, the boat can head you toward it, then swerve off. When you drop the handle you should have enough momentum to carry you right up to the ramp or beach on your skis. Or if there is no ramp, you can glide in parallel to the beach for a stop in shallow water.

The "sit on dock" is another effective way to come in. Have the boat come in close to the dock and in a course parallel to it. At normal skiing speed, you can figure that your momentum will carry you about 20 feet after you drop the rope. With the right timing you can glide in to the dock, then turn just as you reach it, and sit down. If you find yourself coming in too fast, you can cut your speed by sitting down on the skis and dragging your hands in the water for a somewhat less graceful landing.

Saucer Riding

The new and popular sport of saucer riding offers many of the thrills of water skiing, but at lower speed and with the advantage of more stunts than are possible on conventional skis. The saucer is a circular piece of marine plywood, approximately 40 inches in diameter and about one-quarter to one-half inch thick. It is usually brightly painted, both to

The wooden disc used in "saucering" makes possible a variety of "aqua-batics" that would be impossible on water skis.

protect it from water softening and to add a touch of color to the pastime.

Since the saucer has a comparatively large planing surface, it is towed at relatively low speeds compared to water skiing. This makes it possible to enjoy "saucering" behind a boat with a 5½-horsepower motor, and a 10 horsepower can provide all the necessary momentum for "trick" saucering.

To ride a saucer, the standard 75-foot ski tow is used, but the boat speed should be held to about 10 or 12 miles an hour. At higher speeds the saucer begins to flutter, making control extremely difficult.

The Start

To get up on a saucer, you may start from either a prone or kneeling position, remaining back just far enough to keep the leading edge of the saucer from dipping in the water. Then, moving slowly and carefully—the balance on the saucer is tricky—bring up first one knee and then the other until you are balanced on the balls of your feet in a crouching position. Finally, stand with feet slightly apart as in a good water-skiing position.

The saucer may also be started from a dock. Sit on the edge of the dock with your feet on the saucer about 18 inches apart. Lean back before the rope becomes taut, and try to get the saucer moving when the boat jerks you forward. The boat should be moving at a good speed as it pulls you from the dock. Keep a low crouch, back and arms straight, and the front of the saucer well out of the water.

Although there are no bindings on the saucer, it is not difficult to keep your feet planted firmly on it. The pressure of the water pushes the saucer up against your feet, and if you keep your balance it is no harder to maneuver on a saucer than on water skis.

To maneuver the saucer, shift your weight and lean in the direction you want to go. To steer left, lean left; to steer right, lean right.

One of the simpler applause-provoking stunts on the saucer is the turn-around. To do it, start with a turn. Continue applying turning pressure by leaning away from the towing boat. When you reach a backward position, change hands on the handle. Then continue your turn by pulling yourself around from back to front. Your feet stay put in one position on the saucer during this maneuver.

The average skier will do better by staying within the wake of the boat when he is riding a saucer. Even experts have trouble trying to cross the wake of an inboard. It is possible to cross the wake of an outboard during a moderate-speed turn, but care must be observed to keep the leading edge of the saucer from digging into the water.

Despite the tight balance required for saucering, many of

The Skier's Salute: One ski raised out of the water and held vertically is the traditional salute. Here, a skier is raising the right ski to position.

the more practiced experts can perform handstands on the disk, put down chairs and sit on them, even ride them in pairs, or form a pyramid atop a saucer.

The Skier's Salute

One of the first tricks practiced by many skiers as soon as they graduate from the novice class is the skier's salute. Start this by lifting one ski slightly out of the water. Be sure to keep the tip *up*. Hold the ski out of the water until you get the feel of riding on one ski, then lift the out-of-water ski about a foot above the water. When you feel confident, raise the ski to a vertical position in front of you, holding the handle in the opposite hand and swinging the free hand back behind you for balance. Most water skiers find it easier to raise the right foot into the salute position by using the right hand for balance. Try the salute when riding in the center of the wake at first.

Slalom Skiing

Slalom—or one-ski skiing—offers greater freedom and more maneuverability than conventional water skiing. While it is possible to balance for a while on one standard ski, the slalom ski is specially made. It is longer than the standard water ski, has a larger fin and 2 foot bindings, one in the front and one in the rear. The rear binding has no heel support, so that the foot can slide in and out easily. The fin is usually made of stiff metal, and slalom skis are sometimes tapered at the ends.

The start in slalom skiing is practically the same as in a two-ski start, but it calls for a bit more skill. For one thing, in a water start the starting pull will be much greater, because there is less of a planing surface on the one ski and there is more water pressure against the body of the skier. It takes a little more co-ordination to climb up on the water with one ski than with 2. Most slalom skiers prefer to get off from a standing start, and this is the practice in most competition, where the take-off is usually from the edge of a sandy beach. In a slalom start it is important to keep the weight slightly to the rear to prevent the toe of the ski from responding to the first force of the boat's pull by digging in and throwing the skier forward.

Most slalom skiers use the double-handled tow rope in preference to the single handle bar.

Some skiers find it easier to start with one standard ski and one slalom ski. They kick off the regular ski when they are in skiing position, and drag the toes of their free foot in the water lightly to get balance before placing the second foot in the rear binding.

The technique in turning is also slightly different with the slalom ski. As you lean in the direction you want to go,

The single slalom ski is more maneuverable and faster than the two-ski rig. It is longer, has a larger fin and two bindings. The rear binding has no heel support.

you also push the back of your ski around by shifting more weight to the rear foot. On a turn, lean back against the pull of the tow rope, since the deeper fin prevents skidding. One of the advantages of slalom skiing is that on a slalom turn the skier can travel about a third faster than the speed of the boat which is towing him.

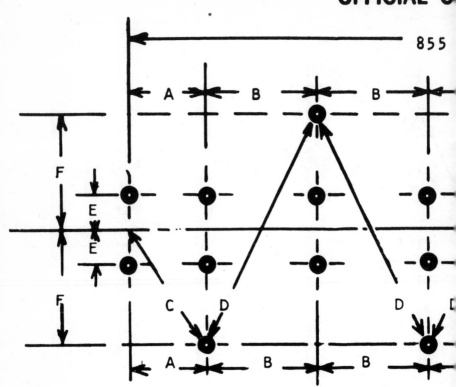

855

DIMENSIONS:

A = 90'
B = 135'
C = 97'6"
D = 154'5.2"
E = 4'6"
F = 37'6"

TOLERANCES:

±½% ON 855' TOTA
±1% ON A,B,C,D,F
±10% ON E

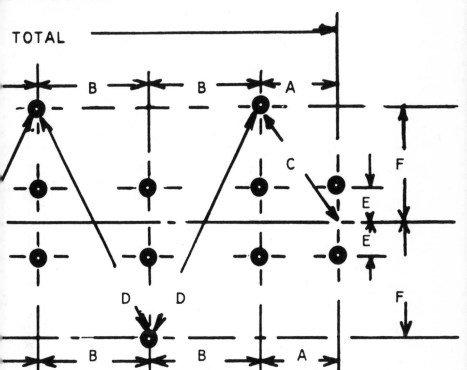

ALLOWED RANGES ON DIMENSIONS:

GTH
855' TOTAL:	850'8.7" - 859'3.3"	
A:	89'1.2" - 90'10.8"	
B:	133'7.8" - 136'4.2"	
C:	96'6.3" - 98'5.7"	
D:	152'10.7"-155'11.7"	
E:	4'0.6" - 4'11.4"	
F:	37'1.5" - 37'10.5"	

Summary of Official Tournament Rules

Rules of competition for sanctioned water ski tournaments are established by the American Water Ski Association, covering the three major events—slalom, jumping, and tricks.

ELIGIBILITY.

Each entrant in a major event in the Nationals must possess a valid Master rating in the event and (except under unusual circumstances detailed in the official rules) must have competed in his Regional Tournament. He also must have finished in the same event in the Regionals among the leaders, as specified in the rules for his division, or among the leaders in the same event, also as specified, in the previous year's Nationals or must meet certain Exceptional Performance requirements.

DIVISIONS OF COMPETITION

Contestants in the three major events are separated into the following divisions on the basis of their ages on January 1 prior to the tournament: Men, 17–34 years inclusive; Women, 17–29 inclusive; Senior Men, 35 and over; Boys, 13–16 inclusive; Girls, 13–16 inclusive; Junior Boys, 12 and under; Junior Girls, 12 and under; Senior Women, 30 and over.

EQUIPMENT

Skis shall not exceed 9 27/32 inches (25 centimeters) in width or be less than 39 3/8 inches (1 meter) long (3 feet for juniors). Any type of fixed foot bindings and fixed fins may be used, but no other devices are permitted.

The jumping ramp is an inclined plane with mounted aprons (safety sides) set at an angle in relation to the jump. It must be from 12 to 14 feet, 1 1/4 inches wide at all points, 21 to 22 feet long out of water, and no less than 2 feet of ramp length underwater. The jump height is set at 6 feet for the Men's Division and 5 feet for all other divisions.

SLALOM

Each contestant follows the towboat through the entrance gate, passes around the outside of all six buoys, and leaves through the exit gate (this constitutes a pass), then returns through the course in similar manner, with the speed increased two miles an hour. If the skier has not missed any buoys or end gates on completion of his second pass, he receives a third and fourth pass through the course. The second run also consists of a maximum of four passes, and all succeeding runs, two passes, until a miss. After maximum speeds are reached, the line is shortened as indicated in the following speed tables:

SPEED TABLE

	Boys Men	Senior Men	Junior Boys Girls, Women Senior Women	Junior Girls
First Run	30-32-34-36	28-30-32-34	26-28-30-32	24-26-28-30
Second Run	36 with 60′ line	34 with 60′ line	34	32
	36 with 53′ line	34 with 53′ line	34 with 60′ line	34
	36 with 47′ line	34 with 47′ line	34 with 53′ line	34 with 60′ line
	36 with 43′ line	34 with 43′ line	34 with 47′ line	34 with 53′ line
Third Run	36 with 40′ line	34 with 40′ line	34 with 43′ line	34 with 47′ line
	36 with 37′ line	34 with 37′ line	34 with 40′ line	34 with 43′ line

Boat Faster

Speed O.K.

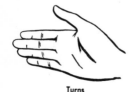

Turns

Boat Slower

WATER SKIING SIGNALS

Stop

Back to Dock

Cut Motor

Distances of over 130 feet have been made by water skiers from the official 5-foot ramp. With the boat traveling at 35 miles an hour, the skiers hit the ramp at about 50 miles per hour due to the speed they gain by swinging. In competition, jumpers are rated on their approach, the ride up the ramp, the time in the air, the landing and the distance.

(Starting speeds for the Nationals are 4 mph faster than those listed unless lowered by a majority vote of the judges.)

A buoy not missed counts 1/2 point when the skier passes the buoy on the outside in skiing position and 1/2 point when the skier returns to within the boat wake before passing the end gate, even if the return to the wake occurs after other buoys are missed. Ties resulting from imperfect runs are broken by repeating the run in which the buoy was missed.

TRICK RIDING

Each contestant is allowed two passes of twenty seconds each through the course, which is approximately 200 yards long. The skier can choose his constant speed through the course. He is scored on the basis of tricks performed (values are specified in the rules), plus form points and a ride-out bonus (if he does not fall in his run). Tricks and form are scored by five judges, with high and low form scores eliminated in determining total score. Each skier is required to file his proposed trick run with the judges in advance, but deviations from the list are not penalized.

JUMPING

Each contestant is permitted three passes through the jump course. A pass or jump is registered when the skier passes the buoys which mark the beginning of the jumping course, except when in the opinion of the boat driver or boat judge a hazard exists because of rough water, interference of another boat, or other reasons.

In the event of a fall after a pass or jump, the skier is allowed three minutes to be back on his skis from the time the towboat returns to pick him up. A jump is scored when the skier passes over the ramp, lands, and skis to the ride-out buoy without falling, provided he does not purposely touch any part of the tow line other than the handle while in the air.

The jumper shall tell the boat driver which side, at what distance and speed (not in excess of maximums permitted for his division) to pass the ramp. Maximum speeds for the jumping event are 35 miles an hour for Men, 28 miles an hour for Women, Senior Women, Senior Men, Boys and Girls, and 26 miles an hour for Junior Boys and Junior Girls.

In addition to distance, jumpers are judged on form by five judges. A total of up to 20 points is awarded for approach to the ramp, ride up the ramp, control in the air, position in the air, landing, and ride-out. The high and low judges' totals are eliminated, and the remaining three totals averaged and applied as a percentage to the jumper's distance, with the resulting figure added to his distance to determine his score. The jumper's highest single score determines his placement in the event.

SAFETY

Mandatory safety equipment and the appointment of a safety director for sanctioned tournaments are emphasized in the official rules. Flotation devices, including lifebelts or life jackets capable of floating the skier, preferably head up, must be worn by contestants in slalom. Approved life vests meeting the specifications for flotation devices plus providing adequate protection from impact damage to ribs and internal organs are required of jumpers. Because of slow speeds involved, the proximity of pickup boats, and the necessity for utmost freedom of movement by the contestant, trick riding rules do not require the wearing of safety equipment.

The tournament safety director is charged with responsibility for observation of all safety measures involving equipment, contestants, and general skiing conditions. He has the authority to take whatever action is necessary, including stopping the tournament whenever he observes a

The heel tow is one of the standard water-ski tricks. The handle is placed behind the ankle, then released slowly as the strain of the tow rope is taken up the ankle.

condition he considers unsafe. He can be overruled only by the chief judge.

OVERALL SCORING

In computing overall standings, the winner of each event is awarded 1,000 points. Each remaining contestant in the slalom and trick events receives points in the proportion of his score to the winner's score. For example, a trick skier receiving a total of 1,130 points, compared with the winner's 2,560, is entitled to 1,130 / 2,560 x 1,000, or 441 points toward overall. In the jumping event each remaining contestant shall receive points in proportion that the square of his score bears to the square of the winner's score. For example, a jumper receiving 150 points, compared to the winner's

180, is entitled to 150 x 150 / 180 x 180 x 1,000, or 694 points toward overall. Scores obtained in running off a tie in tricks or jumping are not counted in overall, and in slalom, only the points scored to the first miss are counted in overall totals.

Barefoot skiing provides a cloud of spray and wins spectator admiration. It is dangerous, calling for boat speeds of 35 miles per hour or over, and either a jump from skis into barefoot skiing position or a difficult water start from a supine position.

The toe wake turn demonstrated.

The one-ski stepover turn demonstrated by Christy Lynn Weir, 1971 world women's water ski champion
Photo courtesy American Water Ski Association

Aquaplaning

Some of the thrills of water skiing and saucering can be found in aquaplaning. Riding the wake of a powerboat on an aquaplane requires a bit less skill than water skiing or saucering because the aquaplane is towed by the boat and the rider supports himself and maneuvers while holding onto a bridle or "reins" attached to the forepart of the plane.

The basic technique of aquaplaning is fairly simple. As the boat starts off slowly, the board lies flat on the water. With the boat still moving slowly, the swimmer comes to the rear of the board and draws himself up on it. He lies flat on the board, grasping it on either side near the front. As the boat picks up speed, the prow of the board rises somewhat above the water. At this point the rider rises first to a

Following the sequence in →
this set of photos of trick
doubles water skiing may
make it seem almost easy.
But even the finale, with the
girl riding in the man's arms,
calls for a high degree of
skill.

In the terminology of water
skiing, a trick such as this is
called a "carry." While it is
most graceful, it can be
quite dangerous at high
speed or in choppy water.

kneeling, then to a standing position, holding the bridle rope. The feet should be set wide apart for balance.

At a boat speed of about 20 miles an hour, the aquaplane provides a rocky, splashing ride, with some opportunity for aquabatics. By pressing down on the left foot and pulling up on the right-hand rope, the board may be made to skid to the right. Reversing this action will skid the board to the left.

The Development of Aquaplaning

The sport of aquaplaning was introduced into the United States around 1919. Visitors to Hawaii had observed surfboards being towed behind powerboats to provide sport when the waves were not right for surfing, and the increasing number of powerboats in America gave some impetus to this new water activity. The first American-made aquaplanes were simply wooden platforms about 5 feet long and $2\frac{1}{2}$ feet wide. They were made very simply. Two or three ordinary boards were cut to size and fastened by 3 cross boards. The cross cleats were placed on the upper side of the plane. The two lines and bridle were affixed to holes cut in the front corners of the boards.

In its heyday the aquaplane provided many exciting water scenes for motion-picture news cameras. Among the leading aquaplaners were the Pope brothers, Dick and Malcolm, who later developed Cypress Gardens in Florida as a water-sports center. Tandem riding, cross rides, shoulder carries and other variations of the basic ride, provided vicarious thrills and goals for amateur aquaplaners. One of the more spectacular stunts was a transfer from riding an aquaplane to a sky kite pulled by another boat, and an air-borne trip before a fast drop into the water.

By the late 20's, faster boats were available to the aquaplaner and the equipment became more sophisticated. Some of the boards were built like toboggans, with an upraised

Aquaplaning preceded water skiing as the "behind-a-powerboat" water sport. The plane is towed by a boat, the rider holding on to a rope "bridle."

The "Look, no hands!" pose in aquaplaning usually ends in a short ride and a wet finish.

front edge. It was found that a narrower board, 20 to 24 inches wide with a pointed nose and a tapered design, reduced drag and gave better stability and maneuverability.

The "jump" was added to the common aquaplane stunts. By inclining the board upward acutely, "kicking" the board, and pulling up sharply on the bridle, the better-designed boards could be jumped clear out of the water. At about 20 miles an hour, a properly designed aquaplane will "plane," skimming the water with just enough "nose-up" to prevent cutting into the waves. The more modern aquaplaner moved his position toward the rear of the board, with his feet about 18 inches from the tail of the board.

Building an Aquaplane

A hollow or balsa-wood board will have a buoyancy of about 60 pounds. The construction of a hollow aquaplane is somewhat similar to that of the surf paddle board described on Page 134. It consists of a frame made of 1- by 2-inch strips of cedar, spruce, or white pine shaped around cross ribs to a conventional boat shape. The frame strips should be rabbeted on upper and lower inner edges to take a one-half-inch marine plywood covering top and bottom. The edge strips and rear rib are of uniform depth, 2 inches. The 3 intermediate ribs are flat on top and flush with the lower surface of the rabbet in the frame. The lower surface of the intermediate ribs, however, is dropped to make the board deeper in the center, and deepest at a point about 8 inches back from the nose. The aquaplane should be 2 inches thick around the edges, but $2\frac{3}{4}$ inches thick at the center of the forward rib, 18 inches from the nose.

The other 2 intermediate ribs are $2\frac{1}{2}$ and $2\frac{1}{4}$ inches deep. Since the board will probably leak slightly, each of the ribs should be notched or provided with limber holes so that the water may be drained from a corked hole in the rear rib.

After the frame has been assembled, the deck is fitted to the rabbet and set up in marine glue or white lead with 1-inch brass screws (No. 6) spaced 2½ inches apart. The board should then be clamped, top down, to a flat surface to prevent warping while the bottom is affixed to the curved ribs. The inner surface of the aquaplane should be primed with white lead before assembly, to limit the absorption of water.

After construction, the entire board may be given a coat of marine paint or varnish, and the edges may be painted a contrasting color.

For hardware, 2 cast-brass screen-door handles are fastened to the upper edge at the ends of the forward rib, for a one-half or three-quarter inch rope pull-off bridle to which the tow rope is attached. A three-quarter inch rope, for hand hold, should be spliced to the handles.

Chapter 2

SKIN DIVING

TECHNICALLY, the term skin diving refers to subsurface swimming in which a face mask is used for clear vision and swim fins or flippers for propulsion. The "snorkel" or breathing tube is an optional piece of equipment. The snorkel usually has an automatic shutoff valve, providing the surface floater or diver with a means of breathing without having to turn his head. Some skin divers also use a "weight belt." This is a standard 2-inch belt fitted with a quick-release buckle to which lead weights are affixed to provide negative buoyancy under water.

In the past few years skin diving has become one of the most widely publicized water activities. Manufacturers have been offering many types of diving equipment, and practically every sporting goods store features it in windows and interior displays. At the same time, popular magazines have been carrying exciting articles about the thrills of underwater exploration. The resultant boom in the sale of skin-diving equipment has had its grim side. As is the case in any sport that possesses a degree of danger, the untrained and the physically unfit who participate are risking injury and even death, and the use of this equipment by very young children is especially hazardous, despite the fact that many toy counters carry skin-diving equipment in sizes to fit the smallest child.

In some areas legislation has been adopted prohibiting the use of various kinds of skin-diving equipment. Silver Springs, Florida, for example has a blanket prohibition against skin diving except for sanctioned exhibitions, and many beach areas have set aside skin-diving areas or have forbidden the sport. There have also been many reports of accidents where children have been using the equipment in the family pool without adult supervision. The Y.M.C.A. and the Boy Scouts of America have been concerned with the problem of the unskilled and unfit skin diver.

General physical fitness is required for skin diving. No one with any unfavorable condition of eyes, ear, nose or throat should undertake it. A perfect respiratory system, clear nasal passages and Eustachian tube with no sinusitis, ear infection, or eardrum imperfection are the basic requirements, because of the water pressure when diving or swimming under water. Earplugs should not be used to compensate for any ear condition, since they may interfere with the adjustment of pressure and prevent the normal functioning of the eardrum as an alarm signal which indicates the lack of adjustment to pressure.

As to necessary swimming skills, the following water ability (without the use of fins, mask or snorkel) is suggested by the Young Men's Christian Association as the minimum for anyone contemplating skin diving:

1. Tread water (no hands) for 3 minutes
2. In continuous movement swim 300 yards
3. Tow an inert swimmer 40 yards
4. Float motionless 10 minutes
5. Swim 50 feet under water without push-off

The Face Mask

The primary purpose of the face mask is to provide clear vision. Without the face mask, distortion would be caused by pressure of water against the eyes. The mask should cover the eyes and nose, never the mouth. While there are many types on the market, the mask should be chosen carefully, with the following points in mind:

The faceplate or window should be of nonshatterable glass. While some masks have plastic windows, these are easily scratched and broken and have a tendency to fog up more quickly than glass. The glass window should be set in a rubber channel with a metal tightening band for secure waterproofing. The mask should be fitted with an adjustable strap, but it should not have to be drawn too tightly to provide a watertight fit. The mask should fit the contours of the face. Slight leaks around the edge can usually be remedied by sandpapering to provide a snugger fit. A soft rubber mask is generally preferable to one of plastic or hard rubber since it adjusts more easily to facial contours and provides a better seal.

The use of goggles as a substitute for the face mask has been found hazardous. They may interfere with the equalization of air pressure; also injury to eye tissue may result, since underwater pressure may squeeze the eyes.

Use of the Face Mask

The proper way to enter water with a mask is feetfirst. A headfirst dive into water with a mask in position over the nose and eyes may force the mask down over the mouth and nose. This can cause a strong suction on surfacing, which the swimmer may be unable to break without help.

The suggested method of entering the water is to hold the mask in hand, enter the water, then put the mask in place while treading water.

First, however, the beginner should practice adjusting the mask on dry land. By pressing the mask tightly against the face and breathing in through the nose, you establish suction which holds the mask in place. By exhaling into the mask, you help equalize the pressure as you descend into the water. First practice in wearing the mask should be in water about hip deep with face above and then below the water.

The inside of the mask window will have a tendency to fog. Perhaps the most practical way of antifogging it is by moistening the inside, then rubbing it with saliva. There are also a number of antifogging cloths available which may work, and some divers use glycerine or other chemicals, or retain a small amount of water in the mask to rinse it.

The Snorkel

When properly used, the snorkel or breathing tube is a valuable piece of equipment for the skin diver. The device is named after the German submarine which was equipped with a device called the *schnorkel* which allowed the motors to "breathe" while the ship was submerged. The diver's snorkel is made of plastic or rubber in a J or S shape, extending from his mouth above the surface of the water while he is swimming. Its main function is to permit the diver to breathe while his face remains in the water. Its use is important when it is desired to keep an underwater object in sight, and it also permits the diver to rest on the surface without exertion. A properly sized snorkel should be about three quarters of an inch in diameter and not more than 14 inches long. The snorkel is usually fitted with an automatic shutoff or float valve to prevent the entrance of water into the tube when the diver submerges. The snorkel is held in the mouth by a molded rubber mouthpiece which should fit easily and evenly, and has a rubber band or strap to hold it in place.

The use of the snorkel is fairly simple. Wearing the face mask and snorkel, all breathing must be done through the mouth. Exhalation through the nose will only be used to equalize the pressure inside the face mask. Before entering the water, the swimmer should practice putting the tube in place and properly adjusting the mouthpiece and head strap. First practice should be in hip-deep water with the face submerged.

The one important skill in snorkeling is learning to blow out the snorkel on coming to the surface, in order to clear it of water. The valve should be checked for proper operation each time the snorkel is used.

We have already mentioned the hazards of using a full face mask that covers the mouth. Some snorkels are actually built in as part of a full face-mask unit. This type of equipment is considered hazardous, since it requires an unnatural breathing routine. It may also cause injury from excessive suction which can be extremely painful and cause facial tissue damage. And there is a chance of dangerous carbon-dioxide build-up in the mask or tube. The snorkel in such a full face mask does not make it safe for use.

The Swim Fins

There is a wide variety of swim fins on the market. The most important requirement is that they fit the foot properly. If the fit is a bit too tight the footpiece can be sandpapered down to provide a more comfortable fit; some swimmers use waterproof adhesive tape for a better fit. Generally, rubber fins are preferred to plastic. The latter are less flexible and may crack or break. The fins should be wet when they are put on the feet.

Walking on land with fins is easier than it looks if a high, lifting motion of the leg is used. The water use of fins calls for a flutter kick, though the motion is slower and broader than in nonfin swimming; a climbing or bicycle motion is also effective. Treading water, the frog and scissors kicks should be practiced with the fins. A variety of different kicks should be developed to help avoid cramps and to strengthen leg muscles. First practice with fins in the water should be

Fins, face mask and snorkel have made the sport of "underwater sightseeing" possible.

while holding onto a kick rail or the edge of a dock or poolside. Flutterboards or surfboards are also good for practice.

Some Safety Precautions

A float or buoy should be used by every individual or group of skin divers. An inflated rubber inner tube painted yellow is highly visible and serves as a resting place, an assembly point, and emergency buoy. The tube should be anchored. In large-group skin diving, one such float should be provided for every 4 divers.

The skin diver's warning flag has been recognized by the boating laws of many states and in Canada. It is a red flag with a diagonal white band, flying from any floating object. The flag signifies to boatmen that a skin diver is in the general area. Boats are required to avoid the area, or if they must pass through it, to do so at very reduced speeds and to keep a sharp lookout to avoid swimmers, floating objects, or passing through air bubbles. Skin divers are required by law to display the flag in some areas.

Hyperventilation—the practice of taking several deep breaths before swimming under water—can endanger life. Repeated deep breathing will not provide the diver with an additional supply of usable air. Instead, this type of breathing may cause a swimmer to become dizzy or even unconscious after submersion. Another effect of hyperventilation is that it seems to turn off the body's built-in safety regulators which normally indicate when it is necessary to come up for air.

The basic safety practices for skin diving are:

Have your general physical condition checked by a physician before undertaking skin diving.

Know the area where you are diving. Avoid murky water or diving amid pilings or other obstacles.

Never dive alone.

Avoid fatigue or chill from too long periods of diving.

Always use a float with line—and diver's flag.

Always enter water feetfirst.

Do not swim under water for long distances or periods of time.

Do not skin dive in rivers with strong currents or in ocean inlets.

Avoid diving in boat channels or where there is any boat traffic.

Always look up when surfacing.

Skill Requirements for Skin Diving

The Boy Scouts of America have established a set of skill performances for skin diving that might well be adopted by any skin-divers' club or by a parent as minimum standards before allowing free use of skin-diving equipment. The B.S.A. requirements state:

1. Enter water feetfirst, holding mask in hand. Attach mask to face and swim on surface for 20 feet, holding breath.

2. Tread water with fins for 2 minutes.

3. Swim 200 yards with fins, using frog, scissors and flutter kicks.

4. With snorkel adjusted, swim for 3 minutes slowly on surface, breathing through tube.

5. Surface dive with fins and mask in 8-10 feet of water and retrieve a 2-pound object.

6. Surface dive with fins and mask in 8 feet of water 5 times in succession, with brief rest intervals on float between dives.

7. Locate brightly colored underwater object from surface, dive and retrieve same.

The Underwater Society of America

In February, 1959, a national convention of skin divers was held in Boston, Massachusetts, and the Underwater Society of America was formed. The goal of the organization is to establish diving councils throughout the United States and Canada to engage in research and to set up instruction and safety programs through local clubs and the national organization. Interested divers may get in touch with the Underwater Society of America for information on diving clubs and the activities in their vicinities. The address is Ambler, Pennsylvania 19002.

Another source of information for the skin diver is the monthly magazine *Skin Diver* with offices at 8490 Sunset Boulevard, Los Angeles, California 90069.

Chapter 3

SCUBA DIVING

THE exploits of TV scuba divers have done much to spur interest in underwater swimming as a participant sport, although "self-contained diving" has been gaining momentum rapidly among water sports since World War II when stories of the activities of military "Frogmen" were released and the equipment became available for civilian use.

The word "scuba," which has become part of the language of water sports in recent years, refers to "self-contained underwater breathing apparatus," or diving using a tank (or tanks) of compressed air strapped to the back, a connecting hose, face mask and flippers. Scuba equipment enables a swimmer to remain under water for varying lengths of time, limited by tank volume and the depth of the dive.

Obviously there is some inherent danger in scuba diving. Because so many persons have ventured into this new activity without the proper skill or supervised instruction and practice, there have been a number of accidents and fatalities. In some areas restrictive legislation has been adopted prohibiting scuba diving or limiting it to certain areas, or requiring certain safety precautions and the display of the skin-diver's flag where diving is being practiced.

The Boy Scouts of America have adopted a general policy that scuba equipment should not be used in scouting under any conditions except in an emergency, and then only by experts. Most experts in the field of aquatic sports agree that only persons eighteen years of age or over should be encouraged to go into scuba diving, and that a long period of training, conditioning and practice under a qualified and certified expert is basic preparation for the sport.

The Y.M.C.A. Program

In 1959, the Young Men's Christian Association started a positive program of training and certifying instructors in scuba diving, and providing such training courses to the public in many of the 700 pools and camps operated by the association. The Y.M.C.A. training program is open to persons seventeen years of age and older. The first requirements are a medical examination, a swim test, and a physical-fitness test which may require some preliminary practice and conditioning.

The swim test (the same as that suggested for skin divers) requires that the applicant for scuba training must perform the following without the aid of fins, mask or snorkel:

1. Tread water (no hands) for 3 minutes
2. In continuous movement swim 300 yards
3. Tow an inert swimmer 40 yards
4. Float motionless 10 minutes. (Survival float may be accepted in case of definite negative buoyancy.)
5. Swim 50 feet under water without push-off

The above might well be accepted by anyone planning scuba diving as the minimum safe standards of swimming ability.

The Y.M.C.A. Course

In conducting the Y.M.C.A. scuba course, a maximum of 16 students per pool session has been set, and generally one instructor is provided for each 4 students. The course includes 16 lessons, 14 hours of lecture sessions, and 18 hours of pool practice and instruction. The content of the courses listed below should give some indication as to the knowledge and practice required for safe scuba diving:

LESSON 1—Lecture, demonstration and discussion: Equipment—skin and scuba masks, snorkel, fins, scuba types including principles of regulator types, protective clothing (wet and dry), weight belts (safety release), knife, compass, depth gauge, watch, and other equipment.

LESSON 2—Water session: Skin diving—use of fins, use of mask, use of snorkel.

LESSON 3—Lecture and discussion: Physics of diving—properties of matter, temperature, pressure, gas laws, density and buoyancy, humidity, illumination and vision, acoustics.

LESSON 4—Water session: Skin diving—recovery of skin-diving equipment, hyperventilation, surface dives, towing buddy, bottom problems to develop underwater thinking, obstacle course, recovery-team search.

LESSON 5—Lecture and discussion: Medical and physiological aspects—direct effects of pressure, pressure effects in descent, "squeeze," gas-density effects, direct effects of pressure on ascent, how much to breathe, nothing to breathe, anoxia, carbon-dioxide excess, carbon-monoxide poisoning.

LESSON 6—Water session: Scuba orientation—hose unit, predive check, tank filling, breathing, hose clearing, harness safety hitch (use with and without a mask).

LESSON 7—Lecture and discussion: Medical and physiological aspects—indirect effects of pressure, nitrogen, decompression sickness, no decompression limits, use of decompression tables, helium, oxygen, what to breathe, mixtures.

LESSON 8—Water session: Scuba doff and don—predive check; filling, review clearing of hoses and mask, doff-and-don scuba hose units.

LESSON 9—Lecture and discussion: First aid and water safety —prevention, general first aid, exhaustion, drowning, air embolism, bends, carbon-dioxide poisoning, carbon-monoxide poisoning, marine-life accidents, artificial respiration, dangerous marine animals.

LESSON 10—Water session: Doff-and-don review and buddy breathing—predive check, filling, review doff and don, "nursing," buddy breathing, towing scuba-equipped buddy 100 yards, towing scuba and skin-dive gear 50 yards after removal.

LESSON 11—Lecture and discussion: Compressed breathing gases—contents of gases, technique of filling cylinders, cascade system description and instructions.

LESSON 12—Water session: Scuba—predive check, filling, emergencies clearing, artificial respiration, review of emergency clearing, perform tube rescues.

LESSON 13—Lecture and discussion: Environment of diving—climate, temperature, surface action, currents, visibility, marine life.

LESSON 14—Water session: Scuba—predive check, filling, perform tube rescue and artificial respiration practice, dark-water diving.

LESSON 15—A 2-hour written test of essay-type questions covering the major points of the lectures.

LESSON 16—A 2-hour water test covering both skin and scuba skills in normal and emergency situations, using standard equipment.

Satisfactory completion of the course leads to a certificate as a Certified Y.M.C.A. Scuba Diver. Advanced training is given in some Y.M.C.A.'s toward certificates as Certified Y.M.C.A. Scuba Leader-Examiner and Certified Y.M.C.A. Scuba Instructor.

Information on scuba training courses may be obtained from local Y.M.C.A.'s or by writing to the National Office of the Y.M.C.A., Washington, D.C.

The History of Scuba Diving

World War II provided the incentive for rapid strides in the development of scuba. In September, 1941, Italian Navy

The modern scuba diver goes to sea with a full load of equipment. In addition to the basic breathing apparatus, undersea hunting weapons and photographic equipment add new dimensions to the sport.

scuba divers dramatically demonstrated its importance and potential military value when they carried out a successful attack against a British tanker at Gibraltar. This attack and others that followed did much to give the United States and British Navies an interest in developing scuba and training scuba divers.

However, the attempts to develop a scuba system go far back in time. There are many reports of different primitive tribes whose divers went under water with inflated bladders full of air which provided an underwater air supply. Man's first self-contained recirculating diving apparatus is probably the equipment designed in 1680 by Giovanni Borelli, an Italian astronomer and mathematician. Crude by any modern standards, his equipment demonstrated man's desire to be able to dive free of encumbrances and independent of a surface supply of air.

The apparatus consisted of a large air bag which fitted over the diver's head. It had a single glass port for vision. Air circulated through a tube running outside, through a smaller bag intended to trap moisture, and back into the air bag. Borelli believed that water cooling would remove impurities from the exhaled air, making it suitable for rebreathing. In order to help the diver regulate his displacement in water, the apparatus also had a complicated cylinder and piston displacement. Although this equipment did not work, it foreshadowed later closed-circuit scuba.

A great stride toward modern scuba came in 1825, when W. H. James, an Englishman, designed a self-contained diving suit incorporating a supply of compressed air contained in an iron reservoir worn about the waist. Unfortunately, this equipment aroused little interest and was not considered important at the time, but this suit was the first to incorporate a supply of compressed air.

In 1866, Benoit Rouquayrol of France patented the first satisfactory regulator for open-circuit scuba. This device constituted a milestone in man's work toward freedom and mobility beneath the sea. The drawback to his equipment, however, was the lack of a suitable supply of high-pressure air such as we have today. As a result, his equipment was developed into a surface-supplied diving suit, and the development of true scuba had to wait.

Then, in 1878, H. A. Fleuss of the British firm, Siebe-Gorman & Co., designed a workable closed-circuit oxygen rebreathing scuba. The unit utilized a solution of caustic potash to remove carbon dioxide from the exhausted gases. In 1902 Fleuss improved the unit in collaboration with Sir Robert H. Davis. This apparatus was the prototype of modern submarine-escape appliances and the forerunner of modern closed-circuit scuba.

BORELLI'S DESIGN

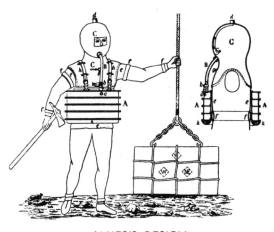

JAMES'S DESIGN

By late 1940, the Americans were in the field of scuba development. In that year, Christian J. Lambertsen developed and demonstrated his oxygen-rebreathing scuba—the LARU (Lambertsen Amphibious Respiratory Unit). This device was first adopted by the Office of Strategic Services, and early in 1942 the first American scuba divers were in training. The same unit was later adopted by our Underwater Demolition Teams for use in operations requiring stealth.

The next development was the patenting of devices for open-circuit scuba, providing a supply of air for the use of the diver, rather than treating the oxygen to allow rebreathing of the same supply. In 1925, Commander Le Prieur of the French Navy developed a self-contained unit with cylinders of compressed air rather than oxygen. The apparatus was basically an open-circuit scuba. However, its defect lay in the fact that the flow of air was regulated manually by the diver. This feature resulted in excessive use of the limited air supply.

The Aqualung

The final step toward a scuba outfit that would meet the needs of water sportsmen came in 1943, when Commander Cousteau, another French naval officer, brought out the Cousteau-Cagan aqualung. This device also utilized cylinders of compressed air, but was equipped with a demand regulator which adjusted the air pressure automatically and supplied air to the diver as needed. Basically this equipment was identical to Rouquayrol's except that it had a much larger air supply. The cylinder of the aqualung held high pressure air (2,000 pounds per square inch) rather than the lower pressure air (500 pounds per square inch) available to Rouquayrol. The greater air supply naturally gives the diver a much longer time beneath the surface. Since 1943 many individuals and companies have developed demand regulators based on Rouquayrol's principles, and with minor changes this type of open-circuit equipment is in wide use today.

Scuba diving is one form of water sport that has commercial possibilities. Propeller and ship bottom inspections are natural scuba functions. Recovery of equipment and almost any form of underwater work are possible with scuba at depths down to 200 feet, although at that depth the underwater time is extremely short. In some areas scuba divers have worked with oyster and clam fishermen. In addition to the sheer enjoyment of underwater swimming and exploration, scuba has added new dimension to spearfishing, underwater photography, salvage and wreck exploration, and the collection of specimens for marine biology study.

The establishment in 1954 of the United States Naval School, Underwater Swimmers, in Key West, Florida, has done much to increase the safety of scuba diving. Many alumni of the school now in civilian life are instructing others in safe scuba diving, and the Y.M.C.A. has based much of its scuba training on the work done at that school.

Psychological Aspects of Scuba Diving

Many scuba divers have compared the "thrill" of their sport to that of piloting a plane. The scuba diver is exposed directly to the underwater environment. He has no contact with the surface and depends entirely on his breathing apparatus and its limited air supply. Even though he is diving with a buddy (a basic rule of scuba diving), he must face most of his problems alone. These conditions demand an ability to adjust mentally to diving. The mobility of scuba diving is perhaps its greatest appeal. The diver has no bulky equipment to hamper his actions. At neutral buoyancy he can swim under water in any direction. He can cover considerable distances unaided, and with the use of any of a number of propulsive devices he can greatly increase his operating range. Depth control is another major advantage

of scuba. There is little buoyancy in the equipment. This
eliminates the need for carrying heavy weights. As a result,
the scuba diver can maintain or change his depth at will.
He can cruise under water at safe depth, can search deep
areas from shallow depths, can explore underwater caves
and travel under ice floes. The water is his domain.

Limitations of Scuba

Any person who undertakes scuba diving should be aware
of its limitation of *duration*. The most important factor in
this limitation is the gas supply in the apparatus. In open-
circuit scuba the gas supply seldom lasts over 3 hours at the
surface, and exhausts in much shorter time at any depth. In
closed-circuit or semiclosed-circuit scuba, the gas supply may
last 4 hours or more, but the absorptive capacitiy of the
canister rarely exceeds 3 hours under any exertion. These
durations are the outside limits. Under normal conditions,
the safe duration of a scuba is 2 hours or less.

The second important limitation is that of *depth*. The
United States Navy has found that in open-circuit scuba the
increase of air consumption with depth limits the apparatus
to 130 feet for reasonable working dives. Nitrogen narcosis
and decompression limit the open-circuit apparatus to 200
feet, even for short dives. In closed-circuit or semiclosed-
circuit scuba, oxygen tolerance imposes very restrictive limits
on depth. Also, scuba limits exertion to some extent. In
open-circuit scuba, the main limitation is breathing resistance. In closed-circuit or semiclosed-circuit scuba it is usually canister capacity.

Some Medical Problems of Scuba Diving

There are certain inherent medical hazards in scuba diving. But knowing them can make it safer, and most of them
can be avoided by carefully observing the safe limits of
duration and by limiting the depth of dives to 100 feet.

Drowning is perhaps the most frequent cause of death in self-contained diving. It can happen for many reasons. The most common cause is physical exhaustion resulting from swimming after surfacing. Other common causes are exhaustion of gas supply, entanglement, flooding of the apparatus, and loss of mask or mouthpiece.

The best measures to prevent drowning are thorough training in emergency procedures, ability to swim well, and the avoidance of panic.

Air embolism—a condition resulting from excess pressure in the lungs—is probably the second most common cause of scuba fatalities. When a man loses his air supply under water, he has an overwhelming instinct to hold his breath and surface immediately. The lack of adequate exhalation during ascent in panic creates excessive pressure in the lungs. This condition has produced air embolism in less than 15 feet of water. Increased lung pressure may also occur in a normal ascent if the diver fails to breathe continuously.

Air embolism may usually be prevented by thorough training in scuba. Learn to avoid hazardous situations and to handle emergencies without panic. Breathe continuously during ascent from depth so that overpressurization of the lungs will not occur. Treatment calls for recompression in a recompression chamber, or the use of oxygen tanks and immediate return to the water so that a gradual return to the surface can be made. However, treatment must be immediate, and in the absence of a recompression chamber, treatment in the water presents many difficulties and risks.

Overexertion is another serious hazard to the scuba diver. Muscular exercise increases the breathing rate and can eventually increase it enough to cause a sensation of inadequate lung ventilation. This sensation can occur even in the free air, and is unpleasant under any conditions. If the scuba restricts breathing, the sensation occurs more readily and also becomes terrifying. The breathing response to a burst of activity may not occur immediately. If the response is delayed, it does not adequately warn a man when he is exceeding his powers. When the response finally does occur, he must stop and pant for some minutes. A period of rest is the best way to relieve the condition. If complete rest is not possible, slacken your activities as much as possible. Remember that overexertion can readily make breathing difficult and that muscular fatigue may not occur before shortness of breath. Untrained divers, especially inefficient swimmers, tend to panic under these conditions and try to surface.

When you engage in any underwater work be prepared for the subsequent shortness of breath.

At depths beyond 100 feet, the scuba diver faces the problem of possible nitrogen narcosis. Symptoms of this condition resemble drunkenness—an almost complete loss of judgment and skill. At the greater depths, fatigue, exertion, and carbon-dioxide build-up increase the susceptibility to nitrogen narcosis.

There is no treatment for nitrogen narcosis. The effect diminishes as the diver leaves the diving depth and vanishes before he reaches the surface. If it is desired to make deep dives, the diver may lessen the effect of possible nitrogen narcosis by exerting strong will power and self-control and by slowing down his activity.

Carbon-monoxide poisoning happens infrequently in scuba diving and its only common cause is contaminated compressed air in open-circuit scuba. Symptoms—the diver's becoming disoriented or unconscious, especially during ascent—may not appear until the diver approaches the surface.

Bring the victim to the surface and give him fresh air. Get him out of the water if possible and give him oxygen to breathe. If he is not breathing, give him artificial respiration. To prevent carbon-monoxide poisoning, you must be sure of the purity of the breathing gas. Keep compressor air intakes away from engine exhausts. The maximum allowable concentration of carbon monoxide in compressed air for scuba use is 20 parts per million, or 0.002 per cent.

Excess carbon dioxide may accumulate in the breathing system of closed-circuit scuba if the absorption system fails, or if the diver exceeds the capacity of the absorption system by overexertion. The accumulation may be gradual. The usual symptoms are awareness of increased breathing, lightheadedness, sleepiness, dizziness, faintness, blurring of vision, and difficulty in hearing. In some instances, rapid increase of carbon dioxide may cause the diver to lose consciousness without becoming aware of these usual warning signals.

The treatment is simple, provided that there is no complication such as drowning. If your buddy develops symptoms at depth, flush his breathing bag to wash out any retained carbon dioxide. Bring him to the surface and let him breathe air. Exposure to the air is all that is required if the victim is breathing. If he is not breathing, give him artificial respiration and administer oxygen. The aftereffects rarely include more than headache, nausea and fatigue.

Another possible problem with closed-circuit scuba is oxygen deficiency. This may occur because the system was not properly purged, or because the supply gas is not pure oxygen. In semiclosed-circuit scuba, oxygen deficiency may be a considerable hazard. The supply contains inert gas, and the failure of the injector system can allow the oxygen to fall to a critically low point.

Here again, the symptoms may only appear during ascent. The diver may lose consciousness, stop breathing, and die if he does not have oxygen in short order.

Under water, give the victim more oxygen in his breathing medium. In closed-circuit scuba, flush his bag with oxygen. In semiclosed-circuit scuba, flush his bag with mixed gas and continue to flush it periodically. He will recover rapidly if he is still breathing. If the victim is not breathing, get him out of the water, remove his scuba, and start artificial respiration immediately. Provide oxygen if available.

Proper maintenance of any equipment in which it can occur will minimize the hazards of oxygen deficiency.

Bends, or decompression sickness, are the result of formation of gas bubbles in the blood or tissue. They will not occur unless a diver comes up too rapidly from depth. The best prevention is to observe all precautions to avoid a too rapid ascent from any deep dive. The symptoms are pain, twinging, numbness, or nervous system disturbances, and the treatment is by recompression in a recompression chamber.

Scuba Techniques

The buddy system is possibly the biggest single safety factor in scuba diving, and the lone wolf in this sport is gambling with his life. Each of the pair of buddies is responsible for the other's safety throughout a dive. The system calls for you to keep continuous contact with your buddy. Where visibility is good, keep him in sight at short range. Where visibility is poor, use a short buddy line to link each other together. Know the standard diving signals and any special signals. Watch for any signal from your buddy. Acknowledge it promptly. Be as alert to help him as he is to help you! If he shows any sign of distress, whether he signals or not, get to him at once. Find out what the trouble is and take action as necessary.

Never separate from your buddy unless he is hopelessly entangled and you *must* leave him in order to get help.

Visual Signals

Communication between buddies and among scuba divers, is by a series of visual signals, although an underwater walky-talky is being developed that will provide diver-to-

diver voice communication under water. The following
are the standard visual signals for scuba divers (see draw-
ings on pages 80 and 81):

HOLD EVERYTHING!—Clench a fist with the thumb extending
across the index and middle fingers. (Fig. 1.)

I AM HAVING TROUBLE WITH . . .—Point with index finger to
the location of the trouble. If the trouble involves equipment,
the buddy must immediately investigate and if possible take
corrective action. For example, if the diver points to his
scuba manifold he may be out of gas. Check to see that his
cylinder stop valves are open and then open his reserve valve.
(Fig. 2.)

ALL RIGHT? or ALL RIGHT.—Touch the tip of the thumb to
the tip of the index finger. Extend the three other fingers,
holding them together. (Fig. 3.)

LET'S GO UP, DOWN, RIGHT OR LEFT.—Close the hand and extend the thumb. Point with the thumb in the desired direction. (Fig. 4.)

PICK ME UP.—Hold one hand out of the water, fingers together and straight, palm toward the pickup boat. (Fig. 5.)

PICK ME UP NOW.—Hold one hand straight out of the water,
fingers together and straight. Swing the hand in a horizontal
circle. (Fig. 6.)

Numerical Signals

In underwater signaling, it is often necessary to be able
to convey numerical information clearly and rapidly. The
following signs are the digits from 0 through 9:

ZERO—Bend all of the fingers into a half circle, holding them
together. Complete the circle by touching the tip of the thumb
to the tip of the middle and index fingers. (Fig. 7.)

ONE—Extend the index finger. Fold the other 3 fingers
lightly into the palm and lay the thumb across the middle
finger. (Fig. 8.)

Fig. 1. Hold everything

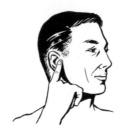

Fig. 2. I am having trouble with my ear

Fig. 3. All right or All right?

Fig. 4. Let's go up

Fig. 5. Pick me up

Fig. 6. Pick me up now

Fig. 7. Sign for 0

Fig. 8. Sign for 1

Fig. 9. Sign for 2

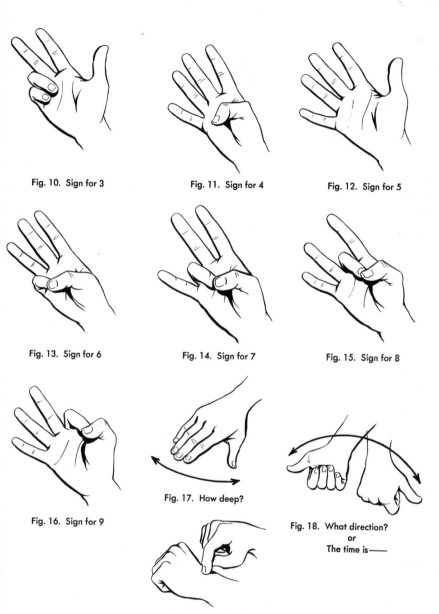

Fig. 10. Sign for 3

Fig. 11. Sign for 4

Fig. 12. Sign for 5

Fig. 13. Sign for 6

Fig. 14. Sign for 7

Fig. 15. Sign for 8

Fig. 16. Sign for 9

Fig. 17. How deep?

Fig. 18. What direction?
or
The time is——

Fig. 19. What time?
or
Compass course —— degrees

TWO—Extend the index and middle fingers, separating them somewhat. Fold the other 2 fingers lightly into the palm and lay the thumb across the ring finger. (Fig. 9.)

THREE—Extend the index and middle fingers and the thumb, separating them somewhat. Fold the other 2 fingers down at the knuckle. (Fig. 10.)

FOUR—Extend all 4 fingers, separating them somewhat. Lay the thumb across the palm to touch the base of the little finger. (Fig. 11.)

FIVE—Extend all 4 fingers and the thumb, separating them slightly. (Fig. 12.)

SIX—Hold the nail of the little finger with the thumb. Extend the other fingers, separating them slightly. (Fig. 13.)

SEVEN—Hold the nail of the ring finger with the thumb. Extend the other fingers, separating them slightly. (Fig. 14.)

EIGHT—Hold the nail of the middle finger with the thumb. Extend the other fingers, separating them slightly. (Fig. 15.)

NINE—Hold the nail of the index finger with the thumb. Extend the other fingers, separating them slightly. (Fig. 16.)

To indicate a number larger than 9, give the individual digits of the number in the order that you would write them from left to right. For example to say "The time is 1435" (use the military time system), you would tap your wrist and give the signs for 1, 4, 3, and 5 in that order.

Other Signals

Certain other signs are valuable for conveying basic information:

HOW DEEP? or DEPTH —— FEET.—Extend one arm to the side, holding the hand palm down. Swing the forearm horizontally back and forth about 60 degrees. (Fig. 17.)

WHAT DIRECTION? or COMPASS COURSE —— DEGREES.—Close the hand and extend the thumb. Twist the hand about the wrist to the right and left several times. When signaling the compass course, always give it as a 3-digit number. For example, to say "Compass course 045," make the sign for compass course, followed by the digits 0, 4, and 5. (Fig. 18.)

WHAT TIME? or THE TIME IS ——.—Crook the index finger of one hand and tap it several times on the back of the other hand at the wrist. When signaling the time of day, always give it as a 4-digit number. (Fig. 19.)

Diving Technique

Before starting a dive, carry out all the preliminary preparations required for the type of scuba you are using. The following is the minimum equipment for safe scuba diving: swim trunks or protective suit (with distinctive band of coloring), life preserver, belt and knife, swim fins, face mask, scuba. Two highly desirable pieces of equipment are a wristwatch and a depth gage. Other accessories that may be necessary are a weight belt, wrist compass and a buddy line.

Enter the water feetfirst, climbing down a ladder or easing over the side of the boat. Do not jump in. Stop at the surface and make the proper surface check for the type of scuba you are using. Check the scuba for satisfactory operation. Check your buddy's scuba for leaks of any sort, and have him check yours. Check your face mask for proper seal to minimize flooding. Adjust your buoyancy.

Orient yourself with available natural aids such as sunlight, current, or landmarks. If you are planning to swim to a specific point, check the compass bearing of that point.

When you are sure that you and your buddy are ready, check the time and start the dive.

Make a slow, orderly descent. Do not try to race your buddy down or outrun him. Swim or pull yourself headfirst down the descending line. Be sure that the pressure is equalizing in the ears and sinuses. Stop the descent if pain develops; level off or ascend slightly until the pressure equalizes. Discontinue the dive if the pressure does not equalize after several tries.

Proper adjustment of the nose piece on the mask is a vital preliminary to scuba diving.

Breathing from the "lung" is one of the first underwater lessons. The instructor holds the lung to give pupil a feeling of security.

The "safety hitch" being demonstrated here allows quick "ditching" of the diving gear.

In an emergency, the mouthpiece of one "lung" can be shared by two divers. Here the pupil learns "buddy breathing."

At Diving Depth

When you reach the diving depth, level off and orient yourself. Use any natural aids that are available such as sunlight, current, bottom, channel, etc. Check with a compass if available.

Avoid underwater exertion and keep your activity to a practical minimum. Breathe continuously, as slowly and deeply as possible. At the first sign of breathlessness, slow down, or stop if possible. Catch your breath before starting any activity. If fighting a current does not let you slow down, break off the dive.

Be especially careful to watch out for entanglement around wreckage, lines or vegetation. When swimming with poor visibility, keep your hands extended ahead.

For free diving wear a comfortable, satisfactory pair of swim fins. Use an efficient kick and maintain a steady pace geared to the ability of your buddy. Watch the depth and time carefully. Keep your buddy in sight and look at him frequently. Signal him before any change in direction. Be sure that he understands the signal and watch that he follows the maneuver.

"Line" diving calls for some cautions. When using a float line, keep it taut, but do not pull the float under the surface. Keep in mind that it can snag objects above you, so watch for entanglements. In any area where there is any possibility of boat traffic, make certain that a diver's flag is firmly set on the float. If you are using a line held by another person, be sure the tender keeps the line taut. Signal him to slacken or tauten as necessary. Keep in communication with him by line pulls. Remember the possibility of entanglement when using a line. Avoid going through any small passages or near snags, and keep your knife in mind for emergency disentanglement.

The Ascent

At the end of time at any deep dive, signal your buddy or the line tender and start for the surface. Breathe continuously and naturally during the entire ascent. *Never hold your breath.*

Do not exceed the rate of ascent specified in the decompression table for the type of dive and equipment. If decompression is necessary, follow the table, using the proper techniques.

The generally considered safe rate of ascent from a dive is 60 feet per minute, and usually decompression should present no problems unless you go deeper than 40 feet. For greater depth diving, you should provide yourself with a United States Navy Decompression Table and follow its directions to the letter. One safe way of handling the decompression problem is to provide yourself with decompression depth markers. A weighted line with knots every 10 feet should work. Weight the line heavily enough to keep it completely vertical in a strong current. An extra air cylinder may be hung at the first decompression stop. If it becomes necessary to surface before getting full decompression, you can complete the decompression by returning to the water.

Know Your Scuba Equipment

Practically all of the scuba in sports use is of the open-circuit type. This type derives its name from the fact that the breathing medium is used only once; the expired gases are discharged into the water during exhalation. Normally compressed air is the breathing medium used in open-circuit scuba, but it is possible to used mixed gases for deep dives. However, oxygen alone must *never* be used in open-circuit scuba.

Once you are under water, your life depends on the operation of your scuba, and you should fully understand its operation before using it. There are two basic systems in open-circuit scuba, the continuous-flow system and the demand system. The demand system is the one currently favored, and is the only one which has approval of the United States Navy. The 3 types which are in Navy use are the United States Divers *aqualung*; the Scott *Hydro-Pak,* and the Northill *air lung.*

The continuous-flow system is somewhat simpler in construction. Basically, it is a self-contained substitute for the ordinary air hose with continuous flow. A simple example is a shallow-water face mask furnished with air from a cylinder carried by the diver rather than from a surface supply through an air hose. Since the flow has to meet the demands of inspiration, and since it continues during expiration, the cylinder must provide at least twice the volume of "breathable" air. This waste will soon exhaust a portable cylinder. In some such scuba, a reservoir bag is arranged to accumulate incoming air during the expiratory phase, to permit larger air flow and reduce waste, and it is necessary to adjust the flow to meet changes in the diver's respiration.

The more widely used demand system provides for periodic release of the compressed air as it is needed for the inspiration of the diver, and shuts off the flow during expiration. A demand regulator controls the release automatically. This is a special low-pressure regulator which maintains the breathing system at surrounding depth pressure, opening to slight negative pressure at the start of inspiration and remaining open only until the end of inspiration.

Parts of Scuba

Open-circuit scuba are generally made up of the following basic components: cylinders, air reserve mechanism, demand regulator, breathing tubes, check valves, mask or mouthpiece (or both), and exhaust valve.

Cylinders

The cylinders, sometimes called bottles or flasks, contain compressed air and are made of either galvanized steel or aluminum. They are specially constructed to withstand the high internal pressure of compressed air, usually 2,150 pounds per square inch for the galvanized cylinders, and 3,000 pounds per square inch for the aluminum cylinder. The volume of the cylinders varies with the different arrangements in use. The general type is a 2-cylinder arrangement, although some European scuba use a 3-cylinder arrangement. The cylinders are usually worn on the back and fastened to the diver by an arrangement of waist, shoulder and crotch straps. A means for quick release of these straps for emergency ditching of the cylinders is provided. The cylinders are fitted to permit easy, rapid replacement of cylinders on the surface or under water.

The Air-Reserve Mechanism

An essential part of the scuba is an air-reserve mechanism to provide a positive warning to the diver when his air supply is becoming critically low. The most commonly used mechanism is an air-reserve valve which permits free flow of air to the regulator until the cylinder pressure falls to a critical level—approximately 300 to 500 pounds per square inch—depending on the type of scuba used. At this pressure the valve restricts the air, causing increased breathing resistance. At this signal the diver opens the air-reserve mechanism, restoring a free flow of air from the reserve air supply. This reserve air supply should be sufficient to allow a safe return to the surface, provided that the dive is not prolonged and that decompression is not needed. The means of opening the air-reserve mechanism varies with different types of scuba.

The Demand Regulator

The demand regulator is a device which controls the flow of compressed air from the cylinders to the diver. An efficient scuba should have a demand mechanism allowing the release of compressed air at a pressure equal to that of the surrounding water and at the rate required by the diver.

The sketch illustrates the basic principle of the demand regulator. When inhalation reduces the pressure in the air chamber below the pressure in the surrounding water, the diaphragm deflects toward the air chamber, depressing the lever and opening the valve on the air supply. So long as inhalation continues, the valve remains open and admits air to the system. When inhalation stops, rising pressure in the air chamber returns the diaphragm to its original position, and the air-supply valve closes.

Demand regulators are of 2 general types, single stage and double stage. The single-stage regulator furnishes the air directly to the diver in a single reduction from cylinder

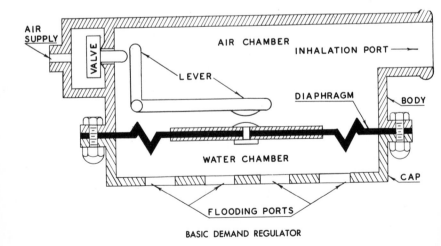

BASIC DEMAND REGULATOR

pressure to a pressure equal to that of the surrounding water. The double-stage regulator is merely a single-stage unit mounted upon another single-stage unit called the first-stage regulator. The first-stage regulator provides an intermediate reduction in the gas pressure through a high-pressure valve to approximately 100 pounds per square inch more than the depth pressure. The second-stage regulator then provides the final reduction through a low-pressure valve prior to the release of compressed air to the diver.

Demand regulators may be mounted either on the cylinders or in the face mask. Cylinder-mounted demand regulators have an advantage in that they minimize the need for medium-pressure tubing, but because of the difference in water pressure between the location of the demand regulator and the effortless breathing point of the diver (at the base of the throat), they make inhalation slightly difficult until the body adjusts. Mask-mounted regulators minimize this water-pressure difference, making breathing comparatively easy and eliminating the need for a mouthpiece.

Breathing Tubes

The breathing tubes currently used in scuba consist of nonkinking, corrugated, or bellows-type rubber or neoprene hose. There are usually an inhalation tube and an exhalation tube. The inhalation tube carries air from the demand regulator to the mouthpiece or mask, and the exhalation tube carries the expired gas to the exhaust valve where it is discharged into the water.

Check Valves

Your scuba may use 3 types of check valves: inhalation, exhalation, and exhaust. The breathing check valves may be incorporated into the full face mask or the mouthpiece, and a check valve is always a part of the exhaust-valve assembly.

The inhalation check valve prevents exhaled air from

Hand signals are used for communication in scuba diving. Here the instructor shows signal for "Okay."

One of the required skills is the ability to clear the face mask underwater. Here the instructor supervises pupil as she uses the proper method.

After a course of lectures and practice, the instructor and pupil dive in a check-out swim.

entering the inhalation tube. Even more important, it prevents water from entering the demand regulator when the mask or mouthpiece floods.

The exhalation check valve prevents water in the exhalation tube from flooding the mouthpiece. Neither of these valves is essential for scuba use, and either or both may be missing from your outfit. However, they do greatly simplify the problem of clearing water from the system.

The important exhaust check valve prevents water from entering the system. All open-circuit scuba must have at least one check valve—the exhaust valve.

The Mask and Mouthpiece

Your scuba may include a full face mask, a mouthpiece, or a combination of the two to provide you with air. A full face mask usually has the demand regulator mounted directly on the mask. Mouthpieces and mouthpiece-mask combinations are commonly used with breathing tubes and cylinder-mounted demand regulators.

Three Types of Scuba Apparatus

The arrangement of the component parts varies considerably among the different makes of scuba. If you are going to use an unfamiliar scuba, the instruction manual should be studied, and if at all possible, some instruction should first be taken from a person who is qualified in the use of that particular scuba.

THE UNITED STATES DIVERS' CORPORATION AQUALUNG: In this scuba, the first-stage regulator, demand valve regulator, and exhaust valve, form an integral unit mounted on the high-pressure manifold attached to the cylinders. The cylinders are worn on the back and are fastened to the diver by means of a harness assembly. They are worn with the manifold up, so that the demand regulator rides the back of the neck. A corrugated breathing tube supplies air from the demand regulator to the mouthpiece. Another corrugated tube carries the exhaled gases from the mouthpiece to the exhaust valve, which discharges the gases to the water. The position of the exhaust valve close to the demand regulator diaphragm minimizes the difference in pressure (water pressure) between the two, so that inhalation and exhalation occur at nearly identical water pressure. The air-reserve mechanism is integral with the manifold and is located above one of the cylinders. It is manually operated by means of a pull rod.

THE SCOTT AVIATION CORPORATION HYDRO-PAK: This apparatus uses a completely different arrangement of components from the aqualung. The cylinders are secured to a back plate which has a shoulder harness for attachment. The cylinders may be worn with the cylinder stop valves up or down. The first-stage regulator is integral with the high-pressure manifold mounted on the cylinders, and reduces cylinder pressure to about 100 pounds per square inch over bottom pressure. A medium-pressure hose supplies this low-pressure air to the demand regulator. The demand regulator is mounted directly into a molded housing on the right side of the mask, which replaces the mouthpiece. The exhaust valve is mounted similarly into the left side of the mask. A special-pressure balancing mechanism subjects the exhaust valve to demand regulator pressure and compensates for pressure differences between the two locations. The air-reserve mechanism on the Hydro-Pak is located in the first-stage regulator and is operated by a knurled knob mounted on top of the first-stage regulator.

The Hydro-Pak contains an added feature not found in the aqualung or air lung. It has a water-ejection button which is used to clear the mask if it should become flooded. This button is located on the demand regulator. Pushing the button depresses the diaphragm, causing a free flow of air to enter the mask and force out the water. Hook a finger under the mask to let the water out in this process, because the pressure-balancing mechanism locks the exhaust valve shut during this operation. The water-ejection button is useful for clearing large amounts of water, or at any time that a free flow of air is desirable. You can clear small amounts of water by tilting the head to the left and draining water through the exhaust valve by exhaling.

THE NORTHILL COMPANY AIR LUNG: This equipment uses the same arrangement of components as the aqualung, with some differences. It has no intermediate-pressure stage because the demand regulator is especially designed to work directly from cylinder pressure. Furthermore, the exhaust valve is integral with the demand regulator diaphragm, and exhaust occurs through the diaphragm from a chamber which is isolated from the demand valve itself. This subjects the demand regulator and the exhaust valve to exactly the same hydrostatic (water) pressure. The location of the air reserve mechanism on the airlung is also different. The mechanism is an integral part of the demand regulator and is manually operated by means of a lanyard attached to a lever.

Sources of Safe Air

The compressed air in your scuba tanks must be free from carbon monoxide, carbon dioxide, oil, vapor and other impurities. Generally, the industrial-type of compressed air may not be safe for scuba use. However, companies which supply compressed oxygen for medical use usually have facilities for providing compressed air. In many localities the local fire department is willing to provide a supply of compressed air from the charging station for the compressed-air breathing apparatus used in the department. Many sports-equipment stores have equipment for charging scuba tanks. Also, there are on the market several makes of light-weight, portable air compressors, especially designed for charging scuba tanks.

Maintaining Your Scuba

All of the scuba equipment on the market is well constructed, but your equipment can be damaged if it is not given reasonable care. If you keep the cylinders, regulators, hoses, tubes and mask assemblies clean, you can expect trouble-free operation for a long time. However, if you encounter any problems that call for replacement of parts or major repairs, it is better to send the apparatus to the dealer or directly to the factory rather than to try to fix it yourself.

The following rules may help you keep your scuba in proper operating condition:

Always stow a cylinder-mounted regulator separately from the cylinders. Never leave the regulator attached in storage.

After use in sea water, thoroughly rinse the regulator and associated assemblies in warm, fresh water. Hang the regulator by its yoke to dry.

Do not allow any water to enter the high-pressure air inlet of a regulator. Insert a rubber stopper into the yoke immediately after detaching a cylinder-mounted regulator. Keep it in place when rinsing. Remove it only before mounting the regulator.

When washing the regulator, pour fresh water into the mouthpiece several times. Make sure that both the inhalation and exhalation sections of the regulator and breathing tubes are well rinsed.

Make an occasional inspection of rubber exhaust valves to see that salt deposits do not lodge around the edges and cause leakage.

Rinse the air cylinders and high-pressure manifold thoroughly in fresh water to remove all traces of salt deposit. Stow the cylinder assemblies carefully when not in use.

Compressed air stored for long periods of time does not show signs of contamination; however, it is recommended that the air be changed at least once a year in idle tanks.

Stow cylinders fully charged. Provide yourself with a pressure gauge and check the pressure occasionally. Keep any tanks holding less than 1,500 pounds per square inch away from places where they may inadvertently be put into use.

Scuba Accessories

The basic scuba equipment is the breathing apparatus and the face mask. However, for safety and comfort in the water, you should consider providing yourself with some of the scuba accessories described here, depending on the type of diving you are planning to do.

LIFE JACKET

Some type of flotation gear is required for use with the scuba. The standard type is a life jacket—an inflatable life preserver—which is a vest-type jacket inflated by a carbon-dioxide cylinder. A tube is also provided for inflation by mouth if the gas cylinder should fail. When inflated, the preserver holds the head well clear of the water. This life jacket should be worn *under* all gear that can be jettisoned. When donning your gear, put the jacket on over your protective clothing, but under the releasable gear such as the scuba and the weight belt.

BELT AND KNIFE

It is a general precaution in scuba diving to carry a knife sheathed in a scabbard on a suitable belt. The knife is your safeguard against entanglement. Secure the knife to the belt with a lanyard to prevent loss. Two satisfactory types of knives are the standard diver's knife and the Army standard combat sheath knife, which are generally available in Army-Navy surplus stores or at sporting-goods shops.

SWIM FINS

Flexible fins for the feet are an important accessory. Without swim fins, you will find it extremely difficult to propel yourself adequately with scuba. The fins are particularly valuable for swimming to the surface in an emergency ascent. Even when diving with negative buoyancy, you should use your fins.

The fins increase the propulsive force transmitted from the legs to the water. For maximum efficiency they should have a large blade and considerable rigidity. Try a few different types to determine which works best for you. If the blade is too large, or if the fin is too rigid, there is excessive back pressure on the fin, which quickly produces fatigue. On the other hand, if the blade is too small or if the fin is too flexible, there is insufficient thrust—again producing fatigue. Comfort is an important factor in the use of fins. Tight or loose fins can chafe or blister your feet. Be sure your fins fit well, and use a larger size over a suit or protective covering for the feet.

DEPTH GAUGE

Depth gauges are designed to be worn on the wrist or attached to some part of the equipment. The United States Navy has conducted tests on various types of depth gauges and warns against placing full reliance on them. However, they do give a fairly good estimate of the depth below the surface.

The two general types of depth gauges are the open manometer type and the Bourdon tube dial gauge.

The open manometer gauge is a flat plastic piece that incorporates a graduated tube. One end of the tube is open, the other closed. On descent, sea water enters the open end of the tube, compressing the air trapped inside. Depth is then read by the height of the water level inside the tube. Poor visibility of the gradations, variations caused by temperature changes, unevenness of the tube bore, crowded gradations, and loss of entrapped air, affect the reliability of this gauge, and its use at depths below 33 feet is not recommended.

The Bourdon tube gauge consists of a spiral-shaped metallic tube with one end open and the other closed. The tube is mounted in a sealed circular case, so that the open end is exposed to sea water. The closed end of the tube is connected by a linkage to a pointer on a calibrated dial. On descent, water enters the open end of the tube and pressurizes the bore. The differential between the bore and the sealed case causes the tube to deflect from its original shape. This movement is transmitted to the pointer by the connecting linkage, and the depth is read on the graduated dial. On ascent, the elasticity of the tube causes it to resume its original shape. This type of gauge is somewhat more reliable than the open manometer type, and if it is protected against possible damage by impact or shock, it should give readings that are accurate within 1 and 3 per cent of the operating depth. It operates satisfactorily down to depths of about 50 feet.

WRISTWATCH

A pressureproof, nonmagnetic wristwatch is essential for scuba use in computing time of dive, controlling rate of ascent and descent, and timing your underwater operations. However, most of the watches advertised as waterproof will not hold up under scuba-diving conditions; obtain one specially made for underwater use.

WRIST COMPASS

A pressureproof magnetic wrist compass is necessary for underwater navigation. Although the compass can only give general directions, because of its inherent inaccuracies, it is a big help, especially under conditions of poor visibility. You may be able to find a naval-type wrist compass at an Army-Navy surplus store.

FLASHLIGHT

A flashlight can be useful in dark or murky water, although its effectiveness falls off as the amount of suspended

Safety—and in many areas local ordinances—require display of the diagonal-striped diver's flag where scuba or skin divers are underwater.

sediment increases. While there are a number of underwater flashlights on the market, they should be used with some caution because of the inherent danger of hydrogen explosions that may result due to chemical action within the flashlight.

LIFE LINES

The *buddy line* is a line 6 to 10 feet long. At night, or in poor visibility, each of the buddies secures one end of the line to himself. The *float line* is a line long enough to reach from the desired depth to the surface. The diver should secure one end around his body—not his equipment—and have someone secure the other end to a float. As mentioned before, the float line may be marked with knots to indicate decompression stops. When diving from a boat use a *surface line*. This is a line long enough to reach from the boat to the point of operation. You should secure one end to your body, not to your equipment.

NOSECLIP

Some scuba divers find that a noseclip is helpful for equalizing pressure in the ears and sinuses. A properly adjusted noseclip is comfortable and does not interfere with pressurizing the separate face mask or with expelling water. It can be valuable for keeping the nose dry if the face mask is flooded or lost. However, you should be able to remove and replace the face mask under water without a noseclip, and a great many scuba divers do not use a noseclip at all.

EARPLUGS AND GOGGLES

The caution about earplugs is: *never use them!* They prevent pressure equalization of the outer ear and cause outer-ear squeeze. It is also possible that earplugs may drive through the eardrum and destroy the auditory bones in the middle ear. If you cannot expose your ears to pressure or water, do not dive!

Never use nonequalizing goggles. They prevent equalization of the eye sockets and cause eye squeeze.

FOOT PROTECTION

If you will be using your scuba around coral, in shallow water, or on the beach, wear lightweight shoes (coral shoes if available) under the swim fins to protect your feet.

Handling Emergencies

Emergencies occasionally arise even though you have taken all sensible safety precautions. They may be caused by your failure to check some item in your equipment, or by some unforeseen or unavoidable development. You can almost always resolve the situation if you and your buddy stop to think. The real hazard in scuba emergencies is not what is happening, but acting on a blind impulse brought on by panic. Few situations in diving are so serious as to require instantaneous action. Remember your training. Do not panic.

Above all, never abandon the breathing apparatus under water unless you cannot ascend without doing so.

EMERGENCY ASCENT

Except in the most desperate situations, make an emergency ascent by *swimming* to the surface. The possibility of becoming entangled or of striking an obstruction makes it hazardous to use positive buoyancy for ascent. Swimming to the surface gives you a better chance to avoid entanglements and to clear any obstructions. Under some conditions a large object overhead may preclude anything but swimming.

An emergency situation can become so desperate that the need to surface outweighs the need for caution. If it becomes preferable to risk entanglement or injury rather than to remain where you are, inflate the life jacket and ascend with the aid of its positive buoyancy. Bear in mind that the ascent will be very rapid. The danger of air embolism increases, and the possibility of serious injury on striking an obstruction becomes great. Use positive buoyancy ascent only in order to resolve a life-or-death situation, and no other. Whatever the means of ascent, exhale continuously throughout.

AT THE SURFACE

When you reach the surface—assuming you have come up by swimming—inflate the life jacket. Decide whether to take off the breathing apparatus or leave it on while swimming to safety.

Your scuba becomes very heavy when it breaks the surface and loses water buoyancy, and the harness may hamper body motion. If the breathing apparatus interferes with swimming, remove the equipment and tow it to safety.

Before removing your face mask, consider the hazards of unfavorable surface conditions such as whitecaps or spray.

FLOODING OF A SEPARATE FACE MASK

Learn to dive without a face mask. Then flooding of the separate face mask is not a serious problem. To clear the face mask use the following procedure:

1. Tilt the head backward.
2. Hold the upper part of the face mask tight against the forehead.
3. Exhale through the nose (another reason why it might be well to avoid use of the noseclip). Water will drain past the lower edge of the face mask.

Also, exhale through the nose occasionally to clear the face mask of small amounts of water. This procedure will also prevent face squeeze by equalizing pressure inside the face mask.

FLOODING OF A FULL FACE MASK

Flooding of a full face mask is a serious problem, but a well-designed scuba with a full face mask has a means of overcoming it. The technique depends on the type of apparatus used. You should have pool experience in handling this problem before undertaking any scuba dives.

FLOODING OF THE BREATHING SYSTEM

The seriousness of flooding of the breathing system depends on the type of scuba you are using. In general, it is less of a problem in open-circuit scuba than in the closed systems. You should, however, be alert to the possibility that the cause of flooding, a cut or torn-loose breathing tube, may prevent successful clearing of the system. Also, you should know how to clear the breathing system of your scuba.

EXHAUSTION OF THE AIR SUPPLY

Running out of air is not a very serious situation unless the air-reserve mechanism has failed to function. Even if this happens, the increase in breathing resistance as the air pressure drops should give you ample warning of this condition.

When the breathing resistance becomes noticeable, open the air-reserve valve and start the ascent. If opening the air-reserve valve does not restore normal breathing, make an emergency ascent. During ascent from any depth, the reduction in water pressure provides at least a small amount of additional air, unless the failure is mechanical.

Continue to breathe normally throughout the ascent, if possible. If not, exhale continuously throughout.

DEPTH AND DURATION GUIDE FOR SCUBA*

DEPTH	DURATION				
	Very Short— 0 to 15 minutes	Short— 15 to 30 minutes	Moderate— 30 to 60 minutes	Long— 60 to 120 minutes	Very long— over 120 minutes
0 to 30 feet	Very Safe	Very Safe	Safe	Safe	Safe
30 to 60 feet	Very Safe	Safe	Safe	Risky	Very Risky
60 to 130 feet	Safe	Safe	Risky	Risky	Very Risky
130 to 200 feet	Risky	Very Risky	Very Risky	Very Risky	Very Risky
Over 200 feet	Scuba should not be used				

*Note: This guide assumes that the scuba diver is an adult in good physical condition and is thoroughly experienced in the type of equipment he is using.

Chapter 4

SPEARFISHING AND UNDERWATER HUNTING

THE second step in the underwater progress of many skin and scuba divers is to take up the sport of underwater hunting. There is an almost infinite variety of game in coastal waters offering many choices of hunting for sea food or for the sheer sport of tracking and capturing sea game.

Any catalogue of underwater equipment offers a wide range of weapons from tridents and lances to rubber-powered and carbon-dioxide-propelled guns, different types of spring guns, slings and harpoons. Some have power heads which fire a cartridge on impact and shoot the barbed spear head through the prey. Some have a break-away feature with a detachable head fixed to a strong cable to absorb the force when a big fish makes his first rush. The exact type of weapon for any specific use depends on the kind of game, the underwater terrain, and the skills of the diver. Basically the underwater hunter's weapons are analogous to those used by the gunner on land. The smaller, lighter-bored weapons for small game; the heavier equipment for the larger marine animals. Also, many kinds of underwater game can be caught by hand.

Basically, underwater hunting offers more of the thrill of stalking and landing the prey than does hunting on land. The underwater hunter must come very close to his quarry. The effective range of underwater weapons is extremely limited. Those which are not used at hand's length seldom have an effective range of much more than 10 feet; and most underwater "shooting" is done at about 6 feet or less. But there is another difference between land and sea hunting. On land the gunner whose aim is successful has only to carry a carcass back to his camp or car. In undersea hunting, "shooting" the game is only the beginning of the hunt. After the quarry has been "shot" the diver must still hold it with a harpoon line, and may have to use additional harpoons to finish it. Very seldom will the first strike kill any large fish, and most will show surprising strength in trying to escape—or even attack when they have been wounded.

Gathering Abalone

Perhaps the most widely known "hunting" activities of skin divers is the gathering of abalones, a large shellfish found only in the water off California and Mexico. Considered one of the delicacies of the sea, the abalone brings a high price in sea-food markets, and is a culinary reward to the diver who brings some up for his own table.

Unlike other common shellfish, the abalone has one shell; the other half of the creature (which is actually a member of the snail family) consists of a strong muscle which clings to its rocky home with great power. The "lore" of abalone divers has many tales of men being trapped under water when the abalone clamped down on a hand or foot, although it is hard to substantiate any of these tales. The tool for gathering abalone is a pry bar which is used to force the abalone free.

Many abalone hunters combine the search for the shellfish with hunting for more active game in the same terrain, as they are often found in kelp "forests" where game fish also congregate.

Hunting Lobsters

Hunting lobsters provides exciting underwater adventure. From Long Island, north through New England waters, the clawed "Maine" lobsters are found. However, their capture is closely regulated by law, and besides limitations on the minimum size that may be taken, most states require that they must be taken only in approved lobster traps or by hand; no weapons may be used. The fast-acting, powerful claws of the lobster make its capture somewhat difficult. More experienced divers approach a lobster from the front. The lobster's characteristic defense pose is to stand on its tail waving both claws above its head. The object is to catch both claws before the creature has a chance to bite. The more timid lobster hunter can approach from the rear, and try to keep his hands out of the crustacean's claws.

The lobster's claws seem to detach from its body almost at will, and it readily sacrifices one claw to obtain a punishing grip with the other, which makes it somewhat of a problem to catch it among rocks or crevices where it often lies with only its claws showing.

Only the Maine lobsters have claws. The lobsters found in other—and warmer—waters are clawless, but protected with sharp spines pointing forward. Projecting feelers act like antennae, to detect any sign of danger, and the response is usually extremely fast—a quick retreat to a crevice or under a rock. Dislodging the lobster is difficult, since its spines give it a firm hold, and it may actually be pulled apart before its hold on the rocks can be broken.

A nocturnal eater, the lobster is sometimes hunted under water at night with a waterproof light. In the open, it may be approached more easily, and while hunting its own food, may be somewhat less alert to a diver's presence.

The Game Fish

In almost every section along the coasts of the United States the divers can find fish that are considered good game. In the northern section of the West Coast, the ling cod, which often reaches almost 40 pounds, and salmon are the prime quarry. Farther south along the California Coast, many undersea hunters go after the white sea bass which travel in schools and reach about 60 pounds; these fish range from a few feet below the surface to about 100 feet down.

In the Gulf of Mexico are found many great barracuda, warsaw, cobia, and the jew fish or black sea bass which reaches some 600 pounds. The Florida Keys abound in game fish. On the East Coast, the sea bass, blackfish, mackerel and swordfish are desirable game. In all waters where they are found, the different varieties of sharks offer exciting hunting.

Sea-Turtle "Riding"

The giant sea turtle of tropical waters is another game that is caught by hand. Underwater, it can easily outswim any diver. The way to capture it is to come upon it when it is sleeping on the bottom; climb on its back, and "ride" it into shore or shallow water where it can be flipped over on its back; a position in which it is helpless. Turtles weighing several hundred pounds have been taken in this manner. Generally the turtle is clumsy and its bulk can be handled by a fairly strong diver. The danger, however, is from its powerful beak which can deliver an extremely damaging bite.

Spearfishing Contests

Spearfishing has become an international sport. Under

the sanction of the American Amateur Athletic Association and similar groups in other countries, competitions leading to national and international championships are held. Teams of three men from local diving clubs are entered in area contests. The top teams advance through regional and national contests to determine the national champions. In the international meets, the top teams from competing countries meet for the world championships.

The use of breathing apparatus is not permitted in formal competition. The rules allow only wearing a snorkel, face mask, diving suit, flippers and weighted belt.

In recent years international competitions have been held in the Bahamas, Italy, Spain, France, Yugoslavia and Portugal.

Information on underwater hunting groups may be obtained from the Underwater Society of America, whose address is Ambler, Pennsylvania 19002. The international governing body is the Confédération Mondiale des Activités Subaquatiques (International Underwater Confederation). Its membership includes the United States, West Germany, Belgium, Brazil, Spain, France, Great Britain, Greece, Malta, Holland, Italy, Monaco, Poland, Portugal, Austria, Morocco, Finland, and the Soviet Union.

Conservation Work

An interesting offshoot of underwater hunting is the aid that skin and scuba divers have given to conservation. In several areas on New York's Long Island, underwater hunters have been found to be the most efficient means of combating the starfish which devour beds of shellfish. Each year divers are called on to join in a mass attack on starfish. Scores of divers respond, tons of starfish are removed from the water, and prizes are awarded to the divers bringing up the largest numbers.

Chapter 5

UNDERWATER PHOTOGRAPHY

WITH almost three quarters of a million Americans finding their favorite pastime in underwater diving and marine exploration, there has been a tremendous increase in underwater photography as a hobby. Several years ago underwater photography was limited to the rather tame technique of taking photographs through the glass-bottomed boats that were features of some resort areas. Today both skin and scuba divers have found that modern underwater camera equipment has added a new element to their sport.

Deep diving has a peculiar psychological effect—the deeper a diver descends, the poorer his powers of observation become, and an image on photographic film is one definite way of recording what he has seen.

The problems of underwater photography were first approached on a large scale by professional motion-picture producers who found considerable public interest in scenes shot beneath the surface of the water. The use of cumbersome diving bells proved both expensive and inefficient and it became necessary to develop truly portable photographic equipment. The first attempts were along the lines of "breathing" equipment, which automatically maintained within the camera housing a pressure slightly higher than the surrounding pressure. In turn this called for pressure

113

regulators and exhaust valves, in order to equalize the pressure at different depths. Later developments, however, made this type of equipment obsolete, and a more modern approach led to the manufacture of pressure-resistant housings with the controls working through self-sealing gaskets. Paralleling the Hollywood work on underwater photography, much research in this field has been done by the United States Navy, although much of the Navy's research has been kept in the "classified" category and has not been made available to the public.

The basic problem of "housing" camera equipment has been approached in several ways. The most simple consists of a flexible plastic bag with about a 6-inch plastic window. For use with most 35mm or simple brownie-type cameras this has been found effective in shallow depths down to about 10 or 15 feet. Controls are manipulated through the sides of the bag.

There are a large number of special "underwater" cameras on the market, ranging in price upwards from $19.95. In addition, underwater housings are available for most popular types of still and motion-picture cameras, in metal—usually cast aluminum—or plastic, generally plexiglass.

Metal housing is usually suggested for divers planning deep work, or those whose equipment will take much abuse. The plastic housing is most often a custom-made job. It allows viewing of all settings on the camera, and more controls can be set in a plastic housing than in most metal ones. Generally plastic housings are tested for depths down to 60 feet, metal housings to about 150 feet. The housings can be built for negative, positive, or neutral buoyancy in water, although many underwater photographers have found that a slight negative buoyancy is more practical. It is somewhat easier to recover a dropped camera that is sinking than one that is drifting upward.

Even subminiature fans have been considered, and there

are underwater housings available for Minox-type cameras. The recent development of electric-eye cameras has made the task of underwater photography easier, and both electric-eye still and motion-picture underwater equipment is available. Electric-eye cameras require a shutter-release control, and if they are not electrically driven, also a wind control. It has been found, in practice, that the automatic-aperture control works effectively under water, as a solution to the somewhat difficult exposure problem.

Underwater Exposures

Exposure settings for underwater photography depend on so many variable factors that it is hardly possible to make specific recommendations that will be generally useful. Among other considerations, the exposures in any situation will depend on weather conditions, the angle of the sun, the clarity of the water, the distance of the subject below the surface, and the color of the bottom. One do-it-yourself way to determine exposures is to seal a light meter in a waterproof jar and take it under for a reading; and there are a number of special "underwater" light meters, and housings are available for most standard light meters. As is so frequently the case in specialized applications of photography, it will be necessary to experiment to determine the best exposure settings for black-and-white and color films.

Underwater color photography presents a number of complex problems caused by the selective absorption and selective scattering of the different colors of light by water. The details will vary for different localities and for various water conditions, but in general red and blue wave lengths tend to be absorbed, so that the light that penetrates to any distance below the surface tends to be decidedly greenish.

Filters

Although daylight does penetrate water to a considerable depth, color absorption and scattering make effective use of natural light limited to the period between midmorning and early afternoon. For depths below 6 feet, it is usually helpful to use a filter to counteract the greenish tinge imparted by water.

For black-and-white film, a medium contrast filter generally gives better results. The Wratten is satisfactory for most waters and has about a 2-time factor or one stop when used with panchromatic black-and-white film. Excessive blues and greens have to be held back to allow reds, browns and yellows to receive their proper share in the color balance. With a filter, the maximum camera range through water is about 40 feet. The greater the distance through water, the more filtering is required, resulting in a denser filter to compensate. At present it appears that until faster color film is available, distances greater than approximately 40 feet through water are impractical to filter. The important fact to have in mind for using underwater color filters is the light distance *through* water. This involves both distance and depth. For example, if your depth is 5 feet and your object is 15 feet from the camera, your light distance *through* water is 20 feet.

An underwater color filter with a factor of approximately 2 times or one stop is effective up to about 20 feet through water. One with a factor of approximately 4 times, or 2 stops, is effective from about 20 feet to 40 feet. Those factors cover daylight-type color film. Distances beyond 40 feet will be aided considerably by the use of a filter, if light is sufficient to bring them in. It has been found that results are better if the background of the underwater picture is held to within 40 feet. In underwater photography it is important to "background" your photographs. Better results will be obtained if the subject is "shot" against coral or other background within the effective camera range. Do not shoot into a water mass.

Underwater filters are made of plastic and are moderately

Scuba equipment and the plastic-encased underwater camera have opened new vistas for amateur and professional photographers.

stable, but should be kept out of direct sunlight and covered when not in use. The filters can be used on underwater cameras with filter mounts on the outside. Wash them with fresh water after using. They are susceptible to scratches, but small scratches will not interfere when used under water on the outside of a camera case.

In discussing filters, it is necessary to speak in approximations in some cases. The use of filters under water (the same as in air) will vary with surrounding conditions. Under water, they are: turbidity, sunlight and clouds, and particularly the color of the water. The judgment gained by experience will be of value in selecting filters as well as other photographic settings.

For the ultratechnical expert, the underwater filter should be changed to a small degree according to the water color found in each location each day, and possibly each hour. However, for general use the filters described above should satisfactorily cover the greatest number of underwater situations.

Color Shots

Except in very clear water, the light that does penetrate is generally strongly scattered, so that it produces a colored haze or cloudiness between the camera and the subject. Therefore, in order to reduce the effects of intervening haze, it is usually desirable to work as close to the subject as possible. This is especially true in color photography, because the color of the haze quickly overcomes other subject colors.

The color of the water varies from one location to another. In fact, even in one location it can change from day to day or even hour to hour as a result of suspended particles of rock or soil and the kind and amount of minute suspended plants and animals. In certain circumstances the over-all tint imparted by the color of the water can be offset to some extent by the use of color-compensating filters. It is usually not possible to make colors reproduce as they would if the subject were above water, but such an effect is not usually desired, anyway.

Artificial Light

The use of underwater flash should be very helpful, not only because it will, more or less independent of depth, supply more dependable illumination than natural light, but also because it will probably give less trouble from the colored scatter haze. Exposure settings for flash shots will depend on the particular equipment used and is best determined by practical experience. The use of artificial lighting is also important because some of the more tempting underwater scenes will often be in darker spots—in caves, wrecks and similar locations.

Another reason for the use of flash equipment is that the water at some depth is likely to be less turbid than shallow water, providing a better photographic medium but requiring some source of light for effective photography.

However, there are some limitations on the use of ordinary flash bulbs under water. Since sea water transmits only blue and green, it will tend to damp out the light from a magnesium bulb, which is rich in red and somewhat poor in blue colors. Another problem in underwater photography is the need to rise to the surface to change bulbs after each flash. Both of these problems may be counteracted by the acquisition of a somewhat more expensive electronic flash bulb of the stroboscopic type, which will allow repeated picture taking with no bulb changes. It is also better adapted for rapid action shots without the blurring caused by motion of the subject.

Focal Length

Because of the refraction of light as it passes through water, underwater "feet" are only 9 inches long. This means that a lense of normal focal length will produce a slight telephoto effect when used under water. For this reason it is desirable to use a wide-angle lens if possible. Such a lens has greater depth of field, which is useful when shooting under water where it may be hard to adjust the focus with simple "bag-type" camera enclosures. Some special underwater cameras have focus settings calibrated for underwater distance.

Underwater Film

The old adage about "walking before you try to run" certainly applies to underwater photography. It might be best for the beginner in this activity to start off with black-and-white work in rather shallow water with natural lighting before attempting deeper picture-taking dives or work with color film or flash gun.

Any slow panchromatic black-and-white film should provide prints with good color contrast. For color work, the Eastman Kodak Company makes the following suggestions, which apply equally to comparable film under other trade names:

> The use of Kodacolor film has several advantages for underwater color shooting. It has greater exposure latitude than reversal films, such as Kodachrome film or Kodak Ektachrome film. This latitude helps minimize any exposure errors that might be made under the uncertain lighting conditions found under water. Another advantage is that no filters need be used on the camera for correcting the color balance of the film for underwater shooting. Such corrections can be made when a print or transparency is made from the color negative. Kodacolor film is available in sizes to fit almost any camera.

APPROXIMATE EXPOSURES FOR UNDERWATER PHOTOGRAPHY

Assuming bright sunlight and light bottom. A dark bottom may require one or two more lens openings; even so, it may cause poorly lighted subjects. Hazy sunlight will usually require at least one-half a lens opening larger.

Film	Depth	
	2 to 5 feet	10 to 20 feet
Verichrome Pan and Plus-X Pan		
Stills at 1/50 sec.	f/11–f/8	f/4.5–f/3.5
Tri-X Pan		
16mm Movies at 16 F.P.S.	f/22–f/16	f/8–f/5.6
Stills at 1/50 sec.	f/16–f/11	f/6.3–f/4.5
Stills at 1.25 sec.		
Kodachrome Daylight Type	f/4	f/1.9 or f/2
Movies at 16 F.P.S.	f/4.5	f/2

Film	Depth	
Ektachrome, Daylight Type,		
Kodachrome II for Daylight,		
or Kodacolor		
Stills at 1/25 sec.	f/8	f/3.5
High Speed Ektachrome,		
Daylight Type		
Stills at 1.50 sec.	f/11—16	f/5.6

The View-finder Problem

One of the first problems of underwater photography that the novice may discover is that standard view-finders are of little use under water. Specially made underwater cameras are invariably equipped with a frame or gunsight-type view-finder. With a camera encased in its underwater housing, it is almost impossible for a photographer to get his eye close enough to the conventional finder to fix the image he wants to capture. Since he will usually be wearing a mask or goggles, his eye will be removed another inch to three inches from the finder.

Reflex-type view-finders might seem to offer a solution, but they create additional complications. An additional pressure-protected opening in a metal housing would be required to observe the focusing screen or ground glass, and there is the possibility of some distortion through the sides of a water-surrounded plexiglass housing. In addition, there is the problem of clouding up through condensation. The old reliable spit, or soap, can be rubbed on the windows to cut down this clouding. There are also some chemical compounds on the market which may be put into the housing to absorb the moisture, but some of them may dry up the film and make it brittle if it is left in the loaded camera too long.

Generally, the most effective view-finders for underwater

The press-type view-finder shown in use here has proved most effective for underwater photography.

use are the frame-finders similar to those used on press or "sports" cameras, and the smaller gunsight-finders. The frame-finder on the underwater housing must necessarily be of strong construction for underwater usage. With the use of a wide-angle lens, it will often be found that the scope of the lens is somewhat wider than the field of the finder. In using the underwater frame or gunsight view-finder, the sight nearest the eye is centered on the frame through visual alignment. Since the time for setting a camera underwater is limited, many underwater photographers preset their cameras for two fixed ranges—3 feet or so for close-ups, and about 10 feet for longer shooting.

Lenses for Underwater Photography

Aside from the other conditions which affect underwater photography, the fact that air is about 1,000 times as transparent as water creates a condition which makes it impossible to use standard focus lenses or telephoto lenses in underwater photography. To obtain contrast, the photographer must, as we have noted, get as close to the subject as possible. Also, while in surface photography it is possible to set the range for the distance from the lens to the subject, this becomes almost impossible under water. In almost all underwater picture taking, both the photographer and the subject are in motion, in three dimensions in a fluid medium. For this reason, the depth of field should be great enough to compensate for the inability to pinpoint the shooting distance with any accuracy. In surface photography such a condition could be corrected to some extent by reducing the diaphragm opening, but underwater photography needs every bit of light available, whether natural or artificial light is used. Therefore it is essential that the shortest possible focal length lens be used.

In addition, the wider the angle of field, the better the photograph taken under water. Unless the subject is framed against the ocean bottom, coral, or some other underwater object, the resulting picture will lack the frame of reference that makes a good underwater shot.

Many camera housings for underwater photography use a flat window or porthole through which the photograph is taken. This flat surface in front of the lens may cause some distortion outside the central portion of the photograph. This can be corrected by the use of a submarine lens attachment which is mounted into the front of the housing, replacing the flat window. This housing consists of two elements 3 or 4 centimeters apart, with the front surface in contact with the water. This correction lens permits focusing for the real distance of the subject without correction, and considerably increases the depth of field.

For lens use underwater there are two vital considerations and they are of equal importance: the power of the lens and its greatest aperture. About the minimum lens quality for underwater use is 1:3.5 for black and white or color.

The 35 mm still cameras are the most popular for underwater use, and the lenses that have proved most effective with them are 30 mm maximum for 24 x 24 mm and not more than 35 mm wide-angle lenses for 24 x 36 mm. For use in 16 mm motion-picture cameras, wide-angle lenses 12.5 to 9 mm focal length have worked out best.

Some Cautions on Underwater Photography and Equipment

The skin or scuba diver who is contemplating underwater photography must consider the effect of his photographic equipment on his underwater mobility. The weight of sea water is about 800 times that of air. While the diver with any experience has adapted himself to this medium, he may not realize the extra "drag" of his camera against the water. Even a fairly small camera housing with a flat surface will slow down his underwater progress considerably. In fact, many professional and semiprofessional underwater photographers use power packs to compensate for the drag of their photographic equipment. At any considerable depth the extra exertion required to move the camera through water may exceed the amount of air that can be provided by the aqualung or other breathing device. A smaller stream-lined camera housing may be considered in place of a larger rectangular model. Another inherent hazard is found in the plastic bag-type housings which may "explode" if carried down too deep.

Some earlier camera housings were provided with neck straps to allow the diver-photographer freer use of his hands, but it was found that this was potentially dangerous, as the straps could interfere with the hoses, and even the pressure of the case against the diver could be hazardous. The safest types are those with a set of handles and slight negative buoyancy. For adequate safety, the camera housing should have a working pressure of about 100 pounds per square inch and a test pressure of 200 to 300 per square inch.

All equipment used under water should be free from any sharp projections or corners that could cut the diver or tear his suit. The knobs and levers on the camera housing should be large enough to be manipulated under water, and so designed that they cannot snag the diver's underwater gear or cut him.

An underwater writing slate is a handy accessory to make a notation as each picture is taken, to obtain an idea of the limitations and best operating situations for the camera being used.

In scuba diving with camera, one of the greatest risks is becoming so involved with picture taking that you lose track of the time spent under water. Adherence to the diving tables is vital, and keep in mind the additional burden of the camera.

Sources of Information

A number of companies are now supplying various types of equipment for underwater photography. Their catalogues provide interesting reading for anyone now enjoying or considering underwater photography, and also provide helpful information on any underwater photography problems. Some of these firms are:

Ikelite Manufacturing Company
3301 N. Illinois Street
Indianapolis, Indiana 46208

Sea Research & Development, Inc.
P.O. Box 589
Bartow, Florida 33830

Mako Products
3131 N.E. 188th Street
Miami, Florida 33160

Upsi
P.O. Box 26
Marathon, Florida 33050

Eastman Kodak Company has a number of pamphlets and studies on various aspects of underwater photography. For information, write to their Consumer Markets Division, Rochester, New York 14650.

Chapter 6

SURF RIDING

SURF riding—the sport of riding a wave on a pointed board less than 6 feet long—is perhaps the wildest and fastest of water sports. Speeds of up to 40 miles an hour can be reached as the board follows the crests of 20-foot waves, with the rider using a technique somewhat similar to skiing to keep his balance and control the board.

In the past twenty years surfing has become an international water sport. As a tourist attraction, it was reborn in Hawaii during the 1920's and became more popular after World War II. Historically, it was a sport unique to the Hawaiian Islands. Hundreds of years ago the sport was restricted to the noble families of the Islands. Using heavy boards of native woods that weighed about 150 pounds, the young men of the ruling families engaged in spirited surfing competition with high stakes involved. According to island legends, canoes, livestock, and even tracts of land were wagered on a single ride through the surf. When the sport was revived in Hawaii, it spread rapidly to Australia, New Zealand, South Africa, Peru and the Mediterranean. In the United States the first surfers appeared on the West Coast, where the California beaches provided the necessary rolling surf. Another factor that spurred the growth of surfing in California was the vacation "commuting" between that state

127

and the Hawaiian Islands. In the last few years there has
been some surfing in the East, although the possible surfing
areas are limited. One of the favored areas in the East is
Hatteras Island, North Carolina, where coastal reefs provide combers which have the desired characteristics.

For ideal surfing, the sportsman is dependent upon
geography and the winds to provide the setting for his
pastime. The California Coast provides larger waves, built
up by the steady onshore trade winds that blow day after
day and the south-flowing California current. Also, at many
points on the California Coast and in some areas in Oregon,
there are long, submerged reefs several hundred yards from
shore that create the necessary combers for long rides into
the beach. Reefs off points of land send in waves at an
angle that peel off as they hit the shore, building up speed
and power.

Surf-Riding Technique

As in skiing before the days of tows, the hard work is
getting out to the take-off point. The surfer must fight his
way out through the surf against the winds, waves and
currents. A surfboard whirling amidst heavy foam, breakers
and undertow is no companion for a weak swimmer. The
very first step in surfing, getting through the surf with
the board, eliminates all but the fittest from this sport,
making true surfing a sport for the young and muscular. While some of the experts are in their thirties, the
great majority of participants are much younger. One of
the risks of surfing is being "wiped out" by the force of the
sea at the start, and there is also some danger at the more
popular and crowded beaches from the wild boards that
other surfers may lose.

The take-off point is out beyond the reef where the
combers form. Most surfing is done at high tide. Floating
in water, the surfers wait for the break of the second or third

It is truly man against nature in the water sport of riding the combers on a slithering surfboard.

of a set of waves. The proper moment to take off is just ahead of the break, with a turn just before reaching the trough. Then, the idea is to ride away at an angle of about 20 degrees to the face of the wave and about two-thirds of the way down the front "wall" of the wave.

The take-off itself is something like the "push" of a skier on starting a run. The surfer, lying flat or on his knees, slowly paddles inshore, watching the wave over his shoulder. When the wall of water is about 20 or 30 feet away, the board must be driven ahead as fast as possible. The crucial point comes when the wave lifts the board to its crest and hurls it down its face. As soon as the board begins its descent it must be whipped around until it is almost parallel to the face of the wave. The fin at the bottom and rear of the board makes it somewhat easier to maneuver, and the hands and feet can be used as ruddering power. Once riding the wave, the surfer can rise to his feet for the exciting run that may be for a few hundred yards or even a quarter of a mile. Skilled surfers have some control over their course. It is possible to steer by shifting weight fore and aft or from side to side, or by dropping a foot in the water to serve as a rudder. Because of the shape and conformation of the board, it has a built-in accelerator. To speed up the board, the surfer moves forward. The most ardent speedsters even ride the very front edge of the board. To slow down the speed, he moves to the back of the board.

About the most important single maneuver in surfing is to turn the instant you are in the wave. Unless the turn is made quickly, the surfer will be plunged straight into the trough of the wave—a mishap known in the vernacular of the sport as "pearling" or "pearl diving." The board will have a tendency to head for the bottom, and the breaking wave will throw the surfer head over heels or into a forceful belly flop.

This is one of the danger points in surfing. The board— perhaps with a frayed nose from bottom contact—can pop up into the air with dangerous speed. The caution taken by experienced surfers is to stay below the surface until the wave has gone on and the board has settled down in the water. There have been cases of surfers being knocked unconscious by a rising board. Another similar situation exists when a group of surfers meet in a tangle of bodies and boards, known to the surfing fraternity as a "lumber pile" or "log jam." In any group mishap the safe practice is to stay under water until the boards have gone by. The safe practice when a pile-up seems inevitable is to dive off the board and stay below the surface for a safe interval of time.

On arriving close to the beach, there are different ways

in which the ride can be finished. In practice, most surf rides end in a tumble. It is possible to avoid the shore break by moving to the back of the board and slowing down enough to let the wave pass by, or by sitting down on the board. Some prefer to ride in through the "soup," jumping off the board when it reaches 6 or 8 inches of water, and then running ashore alongside the board and up on the beach, like the similar maneuver in water skiing.

Surfing Techniques Illustrated

Dropping In—the initial slide down the face gives a surfer the speed to maneuver across the wave.

The Turn—using the speed from the drop, the rider "carves a turn" on edge, propelling him laterally across the face.

In The Tube—the idea is to maintain position in the steepest, hollowest and thus fastest section of the wave.

The Cut Back—another type of turn that redirects the surfer back into the steepest section.

The Kick-Out—turning the board so acutely as to bring it out over the top of the wave, ending the ride.

Wiping Out—falling and losing your board during a ride. The greatest danger in surfing comes from being in a wave with a loose board.

The Surfboard

The early surfboards were 12 to 14 feet long and weighed 50 pounds or more. Modern boards are usually made of balsa wood and weigh about 25 pounds. In addition to shaped balsa boards, others are made of balsa and plywood, filled with foam plastic for more buoyancy, and the better boards are fiber-glassed like pleasure boats. Also, some surf-boards are made of marine plywood or masonite hulks containing an air chamber for buoyancy.

Some surfers prefer a square-sterned board, although the Malibu board has become popular in recent years. The type of board is pointed at the tip and sharply rounded at the stern, is about 2 feet and 3 inches wide, and is somewhat shorter than older boards, averaging less than 6 feet in length. Its adherents say it is easier to carry, less tiring to paddle, and takes off rapidly on a wave.

New boards generally cost about $160, secondhand boards are available for about $75, and at the more popular surfing beach areas, boards may be rented. A board can be built for about $20 worth of material. (Plans are shown later in this chapter.)

Surfing Competition

The world-wide popularity of surf riding has led to international competition in the sport. Each November the International Surfing Championships competition is held at Makaha Beach, Oahu, Hawaii, and draws entrants from all over the world. The championship events are preceded by a qualifying event. In this the contestants must select and successfully ride 3 waves in a 30-minute period, and are judged on 4 factors: points at which the wave was caught (first, second, or third buoy); length of ride in standing position; skill and judgment in maneuvering board; and sportsmanship.

In the finals, held a week later, those who have qualified must select and successfully ride 6 waves within 45 minutes. The time periods are subject to wave conditions and may be lengthened if the surf is not running high.

There are 4 different categories in the meet: men's, women's and boys' surfboard riding, and mixed tandem riding. The tandem contest is usually the most spectacular. Tandem teams are usually made up of a man and a woman, and the competition is "free style," leaving the maneuvers to the ingenuity and skill of the participants. A team may ride standing, or with one partner standing on the bent knees of the other, or sitting on the shoulders, or standing on the shoulders on one foot, or perhaps even being held aloft.

There are also localized championships at many beach areas. One source of general information on surfing and surfing competition is a magazine, *The Surfer,* whose address is Box 1028, Dana Point, California.

Paddling

The growth of surf riding and the dearth of good surfing areas in the United States has led to the use of surfboards for a variety of water sports. In the Los Angeles, California, region, the game of "Paddle Polo" was developed in the 1930's and became a popular pool activity and spectator sport with interclub competition among a number of teams. The game is played on a water-polo area of 60 by 90 feet, with rules similar to regular water polo, using a special double-end paddle board.

Paddling the surfboards around the edges of coves during the time that waves were not large enough for surfing, led to the use of the boards as surface speed craft for swimmers. In time-tests held a number of years ago in Southern California, some spectacular times were recorded. A mile was covered in 10 minutes 16.7 seconds; 880 yards in 5 minutes 32.3 seconds; a quarter of a mile in 2 minutes 46 seconds; and 100 yards in 30.7 seconds.

Some water sports enthusiasts have combined skin diving with the use of a surfboard, diving for abalone down 12 to 20 feet, stacking the abalone on the boards, and then taking them ashore for an abalone fry.

In Australia the surfboard is an important vehicle for rescue work in the water, being the standard equipment for lifeguards at many down-under beaches. In the United States, the American Red Cross has been urging its use in a similar manner. The American Red Cross Life Saving and Water Safety Manual states: "The surfboard as a piece of rescue apparatus has been for hundreds of years a unique development belonging almost wholly to the islanders of the South Pacific, notably in the Hawaiian islands. Since the advent of the new type hollow surfboard and with the use of balsa wood on the mainland of the United States, and because of its unrestricted usefulness in all waters, whether coastal or inland, it has become a rescue device of universal appeal and interest. As such it is taking its place as an extraordinarily effective piece of rescue equipment."

With the winter season providing better surf riding in some areas, a number of surfers have adopted the "wet" suits of the skin divers and indulge their sport year round. However, the degree of activity required in surfing usually provides enough body heat to make the sport comfortable for most persons in water temperatures down to about 50 degrees Fahrenheit.

The search for a more comfortable way of life has led surfers to try sails on the board as easier than paddling by hand and foot. Surfboards have been fitted with a short-masted leg-of-mutton sail with a long rudder controlled by the feet or with a tiller or cross member. Keel or center-boards provide stability. The increasingly popular "Sailfish" and "Sunfish" sailing craft are basically surfboards rigged for sailing.

Directions for Making a Surf Paddle Board

Material: A lightweight marine plywood; casein-glued 3-ply wood, sold under the trade name of "Weldwood"; or as a good but heavier substitute, one-eighth inch masonite pressed wood may be used for top and bottom.

The sides should be spruce, and the nose, as well as the tail block, white cedar or redwood. Either galvanized or 7-inch marine screws should be used. All joints should be thoroughly daubed with casein glue before nailing or screwing. In putting on the top and bottom, one thickness of three-quarter inch seamstress bias tape should be put between the joints along the sides before final screwing of the top and bottom to the frame. This acts as caulking. All corners, sides, ends and front should be thoroughly rounded.

Three coats of best grade spar varnish should be applied to the board on completion. At any time when, owing to use, this varnish coat becomes cracked, it should be immediately sealed again and thoroughly dried.

The top and bottom should be nailed and screwed to the side on 2½-inch centers. Screws should be countersunk and the screw holes filled with a good grade of wood "dough."

This board will weigh about 45 pounds when completed.

Care of the Board

The board should be stored in a shady place, and the cork in the nose of the board, which is put in for an air hole, should be left out when the board is not being used in the water. Otherwise the air inside the board will expand with the heat of sunlight and contract as the board is put into the cooler water, possibly cracking the board.

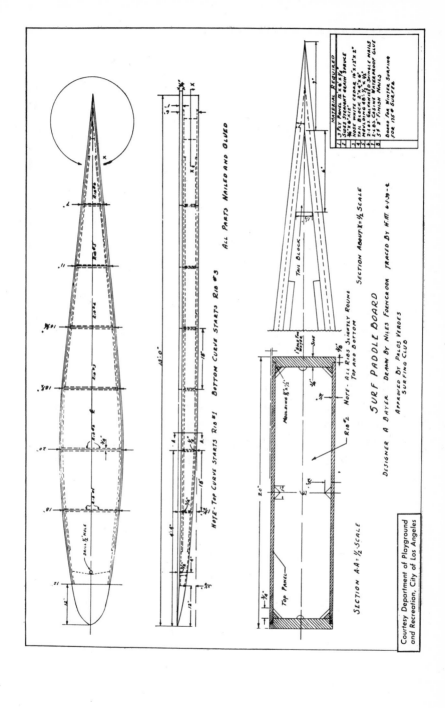

SURF PADDLE BOARD

DESIGNER A. BAYER   DRAWN BY NILES FORNCROOM   TRACED BY H.M. 6-1-39-E

APPROVED BY PALOS VERDES SURFING CLUB

SECTION A-A = 1/2 SCALE

NOTE- ALL RIBS SLIGHTLY ROUND TOP AND BOTTOM

SECTION ABOUT X = 1/2 SCALE

NOTE- TOP CURVE STARTS RIB #1   BOTTOM CURVE STARTS RIB #3   ALL PARTS NAILED AND GLUED

MATERIAL REQUIRED

PADDLE POLO BOARDS: Boards for paddle polo should be made with a minimum width of 22 inches, length of 12 feet, with both ends rounded and flared so that they may be paddled either forward or backward. The air holes should be placed in the bottoms, or a flush countersunk brass fitting used.

BALSA WOOD BOARDS: Many surfers prefer a balsa-wood board for its lightness. However, great care must be taken in shaping these boards. In the professional shops the balsa is glued together in blocks of two-by-fours, carved to shape, covered with fiberglass, and waterproofed with a mixture of resin and a catalyst to give a plastic finish.

"SPEED" BOARDS: The boards designed for paddling with speed are finer, narrower, and longer than standard boards. They run as long as 20 to 22 feet, and as narrow as 12 to 14 inches, with a "V" bottom. Some "speed" boards have also been fitted with light balsa-wood outriggers for greater stability.

Current Surfboard Designs

The current trend in surfboards is to a much shorter board than that used in past years, with a choice of fin systems. The novice might be advised to note the boards that are used in the area where he plans to surf and follow the choice of the more experienced surfers.

TWIN-FIN BOARD

This design is suggested for use on larger, heavier waves. It is fast, and the twin fins help draw the turns out for maximum acceleration. Planned for the surfer who wants to develop a fast running, smooth rhythmic style.

AVERAGE DIMENSIONS: 5'8" x 22" x 4"
                     Width and thickness vary with length.

CONSTRUCTION: 1 7½-ounce fiber-glass top and bottom with ¾-length deck patch and isothalic resin.
                 ⅛" balsawood or ⅙" redwood centerstringer.

FINS: Double Guidance System 6" or single Guidance System 10".

* *Available with diamond or square tail.*

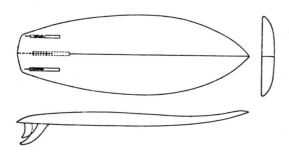

SHORT DECK-SHAPED BOARD

This board was designed for easy paddling and fast response under varying surf conditions and can be had with single, double, or both fin systems.

AVERAGE DIMENSIONS: 5'5" x 22" x 3½"

                       Width and thickness vary with length.

CONSTRUCTION: 1 7½-ounce fiber-glass top and bottom with 7½-ounce ¾-length deck patch and isothalic resin. ⅛" balsawood centerstringer.

FINS: Three Guidance System boxes and two 6" fins or one 10" fin.

* *Available with pointed or round nose.*

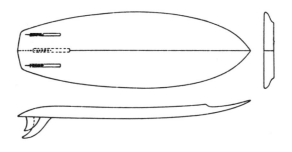

SINGLE-FIN DESIGN

This shape is made for the beach break. It is designed for quick turns and use on smaller, fast waves, under 6 feet or so. Suggested for the skier who likes to turn a lot and drive hard across and through the wave with a quick rhythm.

AVERAGE DIMENSIONS: 5'10" x 21½" x 4"
                                 Width and thickness vary with length.

CONSTRUCTION: 1 7½-ounce fiber-glass top and bottom with a ¾-length deck patch and isothalic resin. ⅛" balsawood or ¹⁄₁₆" redwood centerstringer.

FIN: Single Guidance System 10".

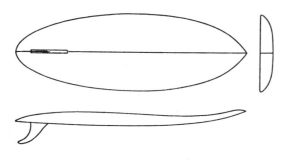

Chapter 7

THE LURE OF WHITE WATER

White-Water Racing

ALTHOUGH it has not received the publicity given to some other sports, white-water racing has a faithful following and is a popular spectator sport in some areas. The International Whitewater Races held at Salida, Colorado, draw contestants from all over the world and often as many as 10,000 spectators. Generally considered the toughest white-water endurance race in the world, it has been held annually since 1948, with the contestants facing a rugged course of over 23 miles in a downriver race. White-water slalom races are somewhat similar to ski-slalom, with the racers swinging their craft between "gates" over a set course in a race against time.

Other regular races are held on the West River in Vermont, Mascoma River (Dartmouth College) in New Hampshire, Loyalsock and Youghiogheny in Pennsylvania, Savage in Maryland, Wolf River in Wisconsin, and the King and Kern rivers in California. The annual race on the Truckee River, near Lake Tahoe, is a popular event.

The 1972 Olympics in Munich found Whitewater Slalom events of kayak (men and women), one-man canoe racing, and two-man canoe events included for the first time.

White-Water Clubs

As in so many water sports, one of the attractions of white-water boating is finding other people with the same interest and joining them in social or competitive river running. The American White-Water Affiliation, 264 East Side Drive, Concord, New Hampshire 03301, is the recognized club in the United States, and membership is open to all who are interested in river sport for dues of $3.50 yearly. This includes a subscription to the quarterly magazine *American White Water*.

The AWA is composed of clubs throughout the world and several in Canada, whose members participate in river running and social activities and also work for legislation to promote the sport and to preserve the rivers for sports use. The AWA affiliates are:

CALIFORNIA

Haystackers Whitewater Club, Tom Johnson, Box 675, Kernville, Calif. 93238

YMCA Whitewater Club, Gary Gray, 640 N. Center Street, Stockton, Calif. 95202

Ballona Creek Paddling Club, John Evans, Rep., 933 North Orlando Drive, Los Angeles, Calif. 90069

Feather River Kavak Club, Mike Schneller, 1773 Broadway Street, Marysville, Calif. 95901

Sierra Club Lomo Prieta Paddlers, Joe Kilner, 185 Loucks Avenue, Los Altos, Calif. 94022

Sierra Club Mother Lode Chapter, Sam Gardali, 914 Stanford Avenue, Modesto, Calif. 95350

Sierra Club River Conservation Committee, Scott Fleming, Rep., 2750 Shasta Road, Berkeley, Calif. 94708

Sierra Club San Francisco Chap., Frances Cutter, Rep., 94 El Toyonal, Orinda, Calif. 94563

John Wesley Powell Boat Club, Charles Martin, Rep., 1329 Henry, Berkeley, Calif. 94709

American Guides Assoc., Box B, Woodland, Calif. 95695

Idlewild Yacht Club, Robert N. Symon, Rep., 3900 Harrison Street, No. 23, Oakland, Calif. 94611

COLORADO

Colorado White Water Association, Mike O'Brien, 2007 Mariposa, Boulder, Colo. 80302

FibArk Boat Races, Inc., Emrys F. Samuelson, P.O. Box 128, Salida, Colo. 81201

CONNECTICUT

Appalachian Mountain Club, Connecticut Chapter, Bill and Janet Blaha, 83 North Street, Guilford, Conn. 06437

GEORGIA
Georgia Canoeing Association, Clyde Woolsey, 4725 Silverdale Road, College Park, Ga. 30337

IDAHO
Sawtooth Wildwater Club, Roger Hazelwood, 1255 Elm Street, Mountain Home, Idaho 83647

ILLINOIS
Prairie Club Canoeists, Sneakin Deacon Kiehm, Rep., 2019 Addison Street, Chicago, Ill. 60618
Belleville Whitewater Club, Linda Seaman, Rep., 3 Oakwood, Belleville, Ill. 62233
Illinois Paddling Council, Phil Vierling, 5949 Ohio Street, Chicago, Ill. 60644

INDIANA
American Camping Ass'n., Ernest F. Schmidt, Rep., Bradford Woods, Martinsville, Ind. 46151
Kekionga Voyageurs, E. Heinz Wahl, Rep., 1818 Kensington Boulevard, Fort Wayne, Ind. 46805

KANSAS
Ozark Wilderness Waterways Club, Robert Woodward, 2209 West 104th Street, Leawood, Kan. 66206

MARYLAND
Canoe Cruisers Association, John Thomson, 23 Grafton Street, Chevy Chase, Md. 20015
Explorer Post 757, Nancy Rayburn, Rep., 203 Longwood Road, Balitmore, Md. 21210
Monocacy Canoe Club, David Meadows, Rep., Route 7, Box 371, Frederick, Md. 21701

MASSACHUSETTS
Westfield River Whitewater Canoe Club, Merritt Andrews, Chm., 90 Silver Street, Westfield, Mass. 01085
Appalachian Mountain Club, Worcester Chapter, John Dryden, 125 Grafton Street, Millbury, Mass. 01527
Appalachian Mountain Club, Boston, Biff Manhard, Rep., 45 Wesley Street, Newton, Mass. 02158
Cochituate Canoe Club, Inc., Guy F. Newhall, Rep., 99 Dudley Road, Cochituate, Mass. 01778
Kayak & Canoe Club of Boston, John Urban, Rep., 55 Jason Street, Arlington, Mass. 02174
Phillips Academy Outing Club, George H. Edmonds, Rep., Phillips Academy, Andover, Mass. 01810

MICHIGAN
Kalamazoo Downstreamers, James Tootle, 6820 Evergreen, Kalamazoo, Mich. 49002

MINNESOTA
American Youth Hostels, Inc., Minnesota Council, R. Charles Stevens, Rep., 615 East 22d Street, Minneapolis, Minn. 55404
Minnesota Canoe Assoc., Box 14177 University Station, Minneapolis, Minn. 55414

MISSOURI
American Youth Hostels, Inc., Ozark Area Council, P.O. Box 13099, St. Louis, Mo. 63119

Central Missouri State College Outing Club, Dr. O. Hawksley, Rep., Warrensburg, Mo. 64093

Meramec River Canoe Club, Al Beletz, Rep., 3636 Oxford Boulevard, Maplewood, Mo. 63143

NEW HAMPSHIRE
Ledyard Canoe Club, Jay Evans, Rep., 201 McNutt Hall, Hanover, N.H. 03755

NEW JERSEY
Adventure Unlimited, Homer Hicks, Rep., Box 186, Belvidere, N.J. 07823

Appalachian Mountain Club, New York Chapter, George N. Thomas, Rep., 24 Barnard Avenue, Oakland, N.J. 07436

National Council Boy Scouts of America, Mart Bushnell, Rep., North Brunswick, N.J. 08902

Kayak and Canoe Club of New York, Ed Alexander, Rep., 6 Winslow Avenue, East Brunswick, N.J. 08816

Mohawk Canoe Club, Gerald B. Pidcock, Rep., Jobstown-Wrightstown Road, Jobstown, N.J. 08041

Murray Hill Canoe Club, Al Hahn, RD 1, Dutch Lane Road, Freehold, N.J. 07728

NEW MEXICO
Albuquerque Whitewater Club, Glenn A. Fowler, Rep., 804 Warm Sands Drive SE, Albuquerque, N.M. 87123

Explorer Post 20, J. H. Fretwell, Rep., 4091 Trinity Drive, Los Alamos, N.M. 87544

NEW YORK
Adirondack Mt. Club, Genesee Valley Chapter, Doug Smith, Rep., 769 John Glenn Boulevard, Webster, N.Y. 14580

Ka Na Wa Ke Canoe Club, Harold J. Gway, 26 Pickwick Road, DeWitt, N.Y. 13214

Genesee Downriver Paddlers, LeRoy Dodson, Rep., Proctor Road, Wellsville, N.Y. 14895

Niagara Gorge Kayak Club, Michael J. McGee, Rep., 147 Lancaster Avenue, Buffalo, N.Y. 14222

NORTH CAROLINA
Carolina Canoe Club, Bob Stehling, Box 9011, Greensboro, N.C. 27408

OHIO
American Youth Hostels, Inc., Columbus, Ohio, Council, Charles H. Pace, 650 Noe-Bixby Road, Columbus, Ohio 43213

Keel-Haulers Canoe Club, John A. Kobak, Rep., 1649 Allen Drive, Westlake, Ohio 44145

Warner & Swasey Canoe Club, Wayne McRobie, Rep., 406 Mill Avenue SW, New Philadelphia, Ohio 44663

OREGON
Oregon Kayak & Canoe Club, Toddy Stanley, 13975 SW Bonnie Brae Street, Beaverton, Ore. 97005

PENNSYLVANIA

American Youth Hostels, Inc., Pittsburgh Council, Bruce E. Sindquist, 210 College Park Drive, Monroeville, Pa. 15146

Buck Ridge Ski Club, Hans Buehler, Rep., 1155 Schoolhouse Lane, West Chester, Pa. 19380

Central Ski Club of Philadelphia, Paul A. Liebman, Rep., 345 South 18th Street, Philadelphia, Pa. 19103

Endless Mt. Voyageurs, Louis Hopf, Rep., 285 Short Hill Drive, Clarks Green, Pa. 18411

Penn State Outing Club, John R. Sweet, 118 South Buckhout Street, State College, Pa. 16801

Philadelphia Canoe Club, 4900 Ridge Avenue, Philadelphia, Pa. 19128

Sylvan Canoe Club, Terry D. Sanders, Rep., 1935 Hampstead Drive, Pittsburgh, Pa. 15235

Wildwater Boating Club, Richard S. Brown, Rep., P.O. Box 77, Pine Grove Mills, Pa. 16868

TENNESSEE

Bluff City Canoe Club, L. Migliara, Box 4523, Memphis, Tenn. 38104

Carbide Canoe Club, Jim Ford, 115 Lehigh Lane, Oak Ridge, Tenn. 37835

East Tennessee White Water Club, Don Jared, Rep., P.O. Box 3074, Oak Ridge, Tenn. 37830

Tennessee Valley Canoe Club, Robert P. Shepard, 4403 Montview Drive, Chattanooga, Tenn. 37411

TEXAS

Texas Explorers Club, Bob Burleson, Rep., Box 844, Temple, Texas 76501

Explorer Post 425, B. Millett, 708 Mercedes, Benbrook, Texas 76126

UTAH

Wasatch Mountain Club, Inc., J. Calvin Giddings, Rep., 904 Military Drive, Salt Lake City, Utah 84108

VERMONT

Canoe Cruisers of Northern Vermont, Mrs. Nan Smith, Shelburne Farms, Shelburne, Vt. 05482

Norwich University Outing Club, L. J. Hurley, Rep., Northfield, Vermont 05663

VIRGINIA

Explorer Post 999, Thomas J. Ackerman, Rep., 610 Mansion Circle, Hopewell, Va. 23860

Blue Ridge Voyageurs, Ralph T. Smith, Rep., 8119 Hill Crest Drive, Manassas, Va. 22110

University of Virginia Outing Club, Box 101X, Newcomb Hall Station, Charlottesville, Va. 22903

Coastal Canoeists, R. L. Sterling Drive, Newport News, Va. 23606

WASHINGTON

Washington Kayak Club, Al Winters, Rep., 8519 California Avenue SW, Seattle, Wash. 98116

WEST VIRGINA

West Virginia Wildwater Assn., Idair Smookler, Rep., 2737 Daniels Avenue, South Charleston, W. Va. 25303

WISCONSIN
Wisconsin Hoofers Outing Club, Steve Ransburg, Rep., 3009 Hermina Street, Madison, Wis. 53714
Sierra Club John Muir Chapter, Tom O'Rourke, Rep., 728 South Oneida Street, Rhinelander, Wis. 54501

AUSTRALIA
Indooroopilly Canoe Club, Box 36, Indooroopilly 4068, Australia

CANADA
B. C. Kayak & Canoe Club, 1200 W. Broadway, Vancouver 9, B.C., Canada
Canadian Youth Hostels Assoc., Maritime Region, Ruth Mackenzie, Rep., 6405 Quinpool Road, Halifax, Nova Scotia, Canada
Montreal Voyageurs, Rene Bureaud, Rep., 360 Barberry Place, Dollard des Ormeaux, Montreal 960, Quebec, Canada

ITALY
Canoe Club of Milan, Italy, Federico Maccone, Rep., Via Sammartini 5, Milano, Italy

The Eskimo Roll or "Esquimautage"

One of the most spectacular features of white-water boating is an Eskimo roll or *esquimautage*—the French term for the maneuver. With a narrow kayak, properly "skirted" to keep water out, the roll-over can be performed in water over 3 feet deep with comparative safety.

Experts in the field say that preliminary practice in a pool, wearing a face mask, is helpful in enabling the novice to conquer the natural fear of being under water and in observing the position of the paddle relative to the boat while under water.

An important part of this maneuver is preparing for the underwater roll by taking a fast, deep breath. Many white-water boaters make a practice of taking a deep breath whenever leaning over in the boat, trying a new stroke, or going through waves. After some skill is acquired, the mask and noseclips are discarded, so that when an unexpected roll is encountered, the water hitting the boatman's face will not temporarily stun him.

In the slalom race, white-water enthusiasts ride their craft through a series of suspended gates in a race against time—and the hazards of the river.

The Forward Brace

The paddle stroke used in the roll is called the "forward brace." This is very much like a forward stroke, except that the boat is leaned, so the paddler's efforts go to raise the boat rather than propel it.

The paddle is inserted near the bow and swept out wide to about 90 degrees from the seat. The arms are kept high, the paddle is extended, and the paddler leans into the brace.

As the kayak rolls over, the paddle should be gripped very firmly, as it will be entirely under water and the force of the water may be strong enough to tear it away. The "screw" roll is increased in effectiveness if one hand is slid along the shaft of the paddle to the neck where the blade starts. It is important to know the exact angle of the blades. If the paddler is overturned in a far-out position, it may be necessary to pull the paddle forcefully alongside his boat.

Once the paddles are alongside the boat and the blades are at the correct angle, the roll-over can be completed. The

more experienced boatmen use the force of the river current to aid in the execution of the roll. It is easy to roll up
in a fast river when going downstream. As the body hits
the water, it creates resistance, thereby slowing down the
boat's speed. Since the water is now going faster than the
boat, the force of the onrushing water on the blade—which
is set at a climbing angle—tends to provide additional lift.

When facing upstream, for instance when crossing a current, the easier roll would be down on the upstream side
of the boat; roll up on the downstream side. Again, the
faster moving water will tend to lift up the boat.

In the fast roll the boatman's face is underwater for less
than two seconds; so that even on a short breath it is possible to try at least two rolls. The important factors in kayak
rolling appear to be knowledge of handling the blade,
proper breathing, and avoiding panic when rolling over or
under water.

Kayak Surfing

One outgrowth of white-water boating is the sport of
kayak surfing, which can also be enjoyed with a canoe.
Even 2- and 3-foot waves present a challenge, and where
there is a higher surf the sport can be as exciting as surfboarding.

One of the problems is to find a satisfactory beach. The
best is a long, fairly shallow, sandy beach with a few offshore
submerged reefs about 4 to 6 feet beneath the surface—a
place where the swells make up steep and come in for a
long distance before the wave breaks. On the West Coast
such conditions are found at Santa Cruz, Rincon, Dana
Point, San Onofre, all in California, and in other beach
areas. On the East Coast there are a number of spots north
of New York City, at the mouth of Long Island Sound, and
at many southern beaches.

As for the craft, an experienced surfer can use almost

any rigid or folding kayak or canoe if he is selective about the time and place he chooses. The most satisfactory canoe to use is a 15- or 17-foot aluminum model. Aluminum is stronger than wood or canvas and resists wear by sand. The longer model seems to perform the best. Next in order of choice would be molded plywood—then a fiberglass plastic —and finally wood and canvas. It is essential for safety to have built-in flotation in the ends. Paddles should be strong oak, ash or maple, and perhaps a bit shorter than those normally used, since they will be subject to great strain—and two extra paddles should always be carried.

For warmth, a skin diving "wet" suit will keep the body warm even on a cool, rainy day. It also acts as a life jacket and protects against abrasion—a few spills are part of the sport.

In surfing, kayaks sometimes have a tendency to slide to the bottom of the wave, burying the nose and sometimes the whole front end of the boat under the water. "Pearling," as this is called, can sink the kayak rapidly. An easily constructed bow piece will eliminate this hazard. What the bow piece does is to provide a planing surface that comes into play the moment the bow starts to go under water. For foldboats it can be made of plywood and tied on with parachute cloth. On rigid kayaks it is fairly easy to make a molded fiberglass nose cone over the front end of the boat, and then attach the planing surface. A three-sixteenth-inch bolt secures it.

A spray sheet or skirt is almost a must to prevent the cockpit or hull from filling with water. On a canoe, a bailing bucket and big sponge are on the must list.

The basic principle of surfing is simple. You merely get the wave to pick up your boat and carry it in toward shore. The wave is a constant hill which recreates itself at about the same speed you slide down it. In beginning surfing it is best to run the waves "straight off," that is—with the boat at right angles to the wave and heading straight to shore. There is a very definite tendency for the wave, as you surf in, to cause the boat to broach to. This action can be controlled by using a stern rudder applied on the side of the boat opposite to the side to which the boat is turning. To be effective the rudder must be applied before the boat has turned very far. Once the turning motion gets well started you may not be able to bring the boat back to the desired right-angle position unless your boat has a large amount of fore-and-aft rocker, and you may break a paddle in trying to do so. You must also be careful not to oversteer. If you turn past the 90-degree point, quickly change and apply the rudder on the opposite side. Actually it has been found that the easiest position to hold is with the boat just a hair off center. If you hold it properly you can go all the way to shore without having to change your rudder to the other side.

To drop the wave you merely remove the rudder and let the boat broach to. If that isn't fast enough, remove the rudder and apply it vigorously on the side to which the boat wants to broach.

There is another problem you may encounter in surfing. Just before the wave breaks, the tendency to broach is magnified and you may find yourself almost parallel to the wave and just at the point where it will break right on top of you. This can be a disconcerting experience the first few times it happens, but is no cause for alarm. All you need do is paddle brace, or if the wave is pretty big, dig your paddle into the ocean side of the breaking wave. If this is done properly, the deck will roll toward the ocean and the bottom will be exposed, with no sharp edges to catch in the water, as you gracefully ride the wave all the way to shore sideways. Experience will show how far to paddle brace. If you roll over toward the ocean, you have braced too hard; if you roll shoreward, not hard enough.

Going in sideways in front of a wave that has broken raises another problem. It is difficult, often impossible, to drop the wave. You may be able to drop it by using a strong combination of paddle brace and draw stroke on the ocean side of your boat, and at the same time shaking (as in a hula dance) and repeatedly rolling the bottom of your boat out of the water. Using these tactics, you can sometimes climb to the top of the crest and eventually lose the wave. If you cannot, and especially if the surf is breaking against a cliff or rocks, don't try to be a hero. Roll over and bail out of the boat before you are too close to shore.

If you feel yourself starting to capsize, particularly in a sideways roll, do not try to fight it. Throw yourself forward on the deck, with paddle held parallel to and on top of the deck, and stay there to minimize the resistance to rolling. In this way, the wave can roll you at will (probably 2 or 3 times) but you avoid the possibility of twisting your hip or back. When the turbulence subsides, merely complete your Eskimo roll and continue surfing.

Catching a Ride

Assume that you have successfully gotten through the shore breakers and are sitting in your craft in the surfing area facing seaward. Suddenly you notice a large swell coming toward you. It appears that the wave will make up steep just about where you are, so you turn your boat shoreward, keeping an eye on the wave that is rapidly bearing down on you from behind.

When the wave is about 5 to 10 feet away, start paddling *hard*, straight for shore. As the wave begins to come underneath you, you will feel the boat begin to rise and pick up momentum. At this point, paddle even harder and throw your body forward. As you feel the boat begin to slide down the surface of the wave, apply a stern rudder to hold the boat at right angles to the wave. If you oversteer and

A typical white-water scene—a kayak making its way among rocks and through turbulent waters.

the boat starts to turn to the rudder side, immediately apply your rudder on the opposite side and bring her back to about 90 degrees, and so on into shore. Just before the shore is reached and the wave breaks, apply your rudder vigorously to broach the kayak, and turn out to sea again.

As you gain in experience you will find that once you have caught the wave you can let your boat turn more nearly parallel to it, picking up tremendous speed and covering much ground. This is called "sliding the wave." To do this you must have a boat with lots of fore-and-aft rocker, or surf your boat well over on its side.

Eventually you will find that you can go almost anywhere you wish on the wave. You can "slide" right, turn and "slide" left, run it off straight, etc. for an exciting water activity.

Canoeing Techniques

Canoeing in the surf can be as thrilling as the roughest and fastest white water. Going out and coming in through even a light surf is something not soon to be forgotten. The thrills of surfboarding and outrigger canoeing can be enjoyed with a standard canoe. One of the greatest water thrills is to guide your canoe down the front of a wave with the spray and foam leaping past your face.

If you live near the shore it is a good idea to know how to use your canoe in the surf as a safety skill and even a means of transportation. A canoe can be used, and has been, to perform rescues in the surf when other boats were not available.

The important canoeists' skills for surfing are the sweep, push and draw strokes, and the J stroke and ruddering. The ability to "feel" your canoe and change your balance with its movement can mean the difference between being part wet and all wet. It will be necessary to change paddling sides without losing strokes, sometimes repeatedly, and very rapidly.

One of the first things you will notice as you look at the surf will be the fact that the waves do not come in at constant intervals, but in groups or sets, each one seeming to be larger than the last one. Then there will be a lull or a relatively calm spell before another set comes in. Also notice that the waves very seldom come in straight at 90-degree angles to the shore, but are angled from one side or the other because of the wind.

Watching the surf, you may notice that some spots look different from others. The waves will not be as large; may not even break; the water may be a different color; there may be a jumble of little waves, or even churned-up sand and debris moving seaward. This is a run-out, rip, sea-puss or offshore current—all different names for the same thing. These currents are caused by the returning action of the waves as they roll back down the beach out to sea through a hole in the bar or reef. They are extremely dangerous to swimmers, but an aid to a boat or canoe in getting offshore.

The location of bars or reefs is indicated by breaking waves or light-colored water somewhat offshore, with rolling waves and darker-colored water nearer shore. Sometimes the only way to get over the reef or bar is to follow the run-out or rip. On most beaches the tide rises and falls approximately twice in 24 hours, giving about 6 hours between high and low tides. This can be important to the canoeist because the surf at high tide may be entirely different from what it is at low tide.

Wind is the other major factor to take into consideration. A light offshore wind, one blowing from land to sea, will make the water smooth, with small waves, ideal for canoeing. However, in a few hours the tide may pick up considerably and a canoe too far out may have a serious problem in getting back. If the wind is light onshore from the sea toward land, the surf will generally be moderate with not too many bad spots. However, if the wind is quartering off the beach, blowing at an angle toward land, a rough, choppy sea can be expected. The set or drift, which is a current parallel to the beach, is caused by the wind. It is important to take this current into consideration when going out and coming in.

Getting Out

First, canoe surfing calls for a two-man (or woman) team and teamwork. Study the surf before setting out. Look for the lulls between the sets of waves, observe the runs or rips, and the exact angle at which the waves approach the beach. If the waves are small enough, you can start whenever you are ready. If there is any size to the surf, wait for a lull or pick a runout or rip current. The important thing is to keep the bow of the canoe at right angles to the waves at all times. If you let the canoe get even a little off this right-angle position, the first wave will turn the canoe broadside and the next will roll it over.

Carry the canoe into knee-deep water. The bowman gets in, keeping aft of the bow thwart, and steadies the craft with his paddle. The sternman stays in the water, near the bow of the canoe, keeping it at right angles and lifting it over the waves. If there is a strong set or current parallel to the beach it will have to be compensated for along with the angle of waves.

When the lull comes, push the canoe out. The bowman pulls and steadies the boat while the sternman quickly climbs in from about waist-deep water. He keeps his normal paddling position; with the bowman back of his normal position, the bow should be so light that it will ride high in the waves, to lift up and over the incoming combers.

The crossing of the waves is the crucial point. Once you get started, keep on going as fast as you can past the first break of the surf. It is absolutely necessary here to keep the canoe at right angles to the waves. You may have to change paddling sides very rapidly and use very powerful ruddering strokes. If the wave is going to break on you, the best procedure is to drive through and hope for the best. In almost any surf, even a light one, you can expect to get some water in the canoe.

If, farther out, you have to cross a bar with more breaking waves on it, use the same approach. You will have a better chance out there, with more room to maneuver, to avoid the first part of the breaking wave, which is the most dangerous, by speeding up or slowing down. Or you may be able to find a run or rip through the bar which will make it quite easy to get out.

Once beyond the last break you can relax a bit, bail out the boat, and return to normal paddling positions. Out on the ocean it is important to keep an eye on the wind. Any increase in wind strength or direction may mean trouble, and if there is an offshore breeze keep close to shore. Remember also that an onshore wind usually means choppy seas.

Coming Back In

The trip back to shore may be a bit wetter than the run-out. If you do not want to ride the surf, use the following method: bring the canoe to a right-angle position with the waves, bow toward the beach. The bowman should return to his position behind the bow thwart. The sternman should shift to a high kneeling position with one leg in front of the stern thwart and one behind. From this position he can move quickly fore or aft as needed to trim the canoe.

The surf may look deceptively light when seen from seaward, but watch it! It is important to move more slowly than the waves. As you come near the break you will feel the stern of the canoe lift. Back water hard and move your weight aft. You must keep the canoe from moving forward with the wave.

After the wave rolls by, move your weight forward and paddle forward on back of the wave. Try to avoid the point where the wave would break on top of you by slowing down or speeding up. This is where keeping a right angle to the waves is most important. If the canoe gets the least bit out of line, even a small wave can roll it over.

Watch for lulls and try to come in with them. When nearing shore, pick a small wave and paddle in on the back of it, not the front.

Another method is to come in with the canoe in just the reverse position, bow out to sea, stern toward shore. The paddlers, in the same position as before, back water toward shore on the backs of the waves—holding or paddling into their fronts. With this method you can keep an eye on the oncoming surf and pull hard into it. It is the way surfmen bring in dories and skiffs through heavy surf.

Riding the Waves

The most exciting—and dangerous—way to get back to shore is to ride a wave in. This takes skill, judgment, knowledge of surf and a little luck. Trim the canoe as for the other approaches, with the weight well aft. Starting well outside the breaking point, pick a small or middle-sized wave as it approaches, and start paddling toward shore so that the canoe is moving in the same direction as the wave and at nearly the same speed.

As the wave comes under the canoe, you will feel the craft pick up and start to skid down the front of the wave. At this point, unless you are highly skilled and lucky, you will lose all control, broach to, and roll over in a welter of foam and water.

Stop paddling, move your weight aft quickly to lift the bow out of the still water in front of the wave, and use strong ruddering action to keep at right angles to the wave. If you don't lift the bow it will sheer off, and at once you will broach.

If the wave is large and steep there is danger of pearl diving when the bow is driven down into the still water in front of the wave. The wave then pushes the stern right up and over for a "pitch pole," which is dangerous to both canoe and canoeists. If the bow of the canoe happens to hit bottom, there is a good chance that your next project will be shopping for a new canoe.

If the wave is steep, the stern of the canoe may be so deep in water that some will ship aboard, and the craft may even swamp—and this may happen as the wave breaks, but you must get wet and still keep your weight back.

Once the wave breaks, it will take very strong ruddering action to hold a straight course. But with some practice you should reach the point where you will be able to ride right up to the beach with canoe and crew intact—and fairly dry.

Chapter 8

COMPETITIVE PADDLING

As a sport, competitive paddling in the United States is controlled by the American Canoe Association, an allied body of the Amateur Athletic Union and a member of the United States Olympic Committee. The types of canoes used in international and Olympic competition have been standardized into the C and K classes. These are light, very fast and tipsy craft of thin plywood, constructed for maximum speed and calling for expert handling. The C or "Canadian" is the racing type for 1-, 2- or 4-man crews using single-blade paddles. The K, or rigid kayak type, is a narrow boat propelled by 1-, 2- and 4-man crews using double-blade paddles.

Divisional, national and international paddling regattas are held yearly for both men and women, and every four years Olympic trials open to citizen amateurs are held. The standard course is a 1,000-meter straightway event.

Sailing Canoes

An offshoot of the paddling canoe is the sailing canoe, which is also raced in competition. The standard racer is a decked sailing canoe, a double-ender, 17 feet long, 43 inches wide, and limited to 10 square meters (107 square feet) of sail area. With its full deck, and equipped with a sliding hiking seat, it can be capsized and righted while under way and can reach a speed of 15 knots.

The American Canoe Association also has a cruising class which takes in wooden canoes equipped with lateen sails, leeboards and steering paddles. Also, C Class canoes can be adapted to sailing, being fitted with mast steps, leeboards, transverse tillers and Marconi-cut sails, usually of dacron. Decked sailers and cruisers are most numerous in the East, while the C Class is found in large numbers in the area around Jacksonville, Florida.

Canoe Clubs

The American Canoe Association owns a thirty-five acre island near Cananoque, Canada, where it conducts an annual "under canvas" camp each August for members and guests. Daily activities include sailing races, swimming, paddling races and novelty events. This has been a yearly gathering for over fifty years.

However, the canoeist who seeks companionship on the water and ashore can find canoe clubs in every part of the country where there is water. Numerous groups of canoeists interested in one or more aspects of canoe paddling or sailing have organized a club, acquired or rented property, put up a boathouse and social hall, and function much like a yacht club. The officers of the club are generally a commodore (president), vice-commodore (in charge of land activities), rear commodore (in charge of water activities), and purser (secretary and treasurer). These officials are known as the flag officers of the club. Members of the board of governors usually double as committee chairmen. The usual committees are: finance, building and grounds, social, paddling, cruising, membership, regatta, public relations, etc. The Washington, D. C., Canoe Club has been in existence for 75 years and a number of clubs have celebrated their 50th anniversaries.

Other canoe clubs own no real estate, but have a dozen or more canoes, a few trailers which carry 6 canoes each— and are usually stored in a member's yard. These groups hold occasional meetings and regularly issue mimeographed bulletins listing canoeing events, passing on club chatter and technical information.

Information on canoeing and canoe clubs is available from the American Canoe Association, 400 Eastern Street, New Haven 13, Connecticut.

II

WATER SPORTS FOR
POOL OR BEACH

Chapter 9

ACTIVITIES FOR THE
POOL OR WATERFRONT

THE burgeoning number of back- and front-yard pools has brought to many American homes the problem once faced only by camp directors and Y.M.C.A. swimming instructors—the need to provide aquatic activities to keep youngsters interested, and at the same time to develop their water skills and limit the possibly hazardous horseplay that may follow when children and water come into contact.

The wide selection of water activities on the following pages includes many which have been in common use in camps and pools for a long time, some which are new, some which may appeal to children, others to adults. An attempt has been made to proceed from simple water stunts for beginners or nonswimmers to group activities for experienced swimmers.

Stunts and games played in shallow water help to give the nonswimmer a feeling of confidence, make him feel more at home in the pool or at the beach, and often serve to make an unconscious transition from playing in the water to actual swimming. The more skilled swimmer will derive greater pleasure from the water after he has learned and engaged in some of the more formal water games, and this outlet may eliminate the need for dangerous "showing off" which is one of the more common hazards of the waterfront.

Fun and Learning for Beginners

Some hesitant beginners may be more likely to participate in the following "stunts" if they are played as a follow-the-leader game in shallow water. With some of the more timid "tadpoles," it may be necessary to stand alongside them and give some support. They should be assured that they can stand in the water in which these activities are tried.

JELLYFISH FLOAT—If a jellyfish can do it, your beginners can too. With chin on chest, knees bent under body, hands grasping ankles, head down, try floating for a short time.

GLIDING—This is good practice to show that water will support a swimmer. Push off from side of pool or crib for distance, face submerged, toes pointed, hands outstretched.

GLIDING WITH FLUTTER KICK—Push off from side of pool, kicking for distance.

INHALE-EXHALE—Standing at side of pool, turn head left, take deep breath, turn face down in water, exhale, continue about 10 times, then try right side.

PUSH-OFF ON RIGHT SIDE—With right arm extended, left arm alongside of body.

PUSH-OFF ON LEFT SIDE—With left arm extended, right arm alongside of body.

FLOAT MOTIONLESS ON BACK— (The novice should be supported with a hand at first.) Face side of pool, push-off on back, arms folded on chest or alongside of body, head slightly back, take deep breath, exhale quickly for another breath if necessary.

PUSH-OFFS:

Push-off, float on back for distance.

Flutter kick on back for distance, eyes looking toward toes.

Push-off on face for gliding, then turn over and float on back without touching bottom.

Push-off on back, then turn over on abdomen.

Push-off on back, arms extended over head, then bring arms down to sides.

CRAWL STROKE AND BREATHING—With toes hooked on edge of pool, head goes right for inhale when right arm makes stroke toward hip, etc.

SINK AND PUSH-OFF—Under water and recover large object placed in shallow water.

UNDER THE BRIDGE—Sink and push-off, go through legs of standing person.

JUMPING:

Standing broad jump into shallow water.

Jump backward into water.

SEAL DIVE—Dive into shallow water from position on stomach.

KNEELING DIVE—Dive from kneeling position into 3 or 4 feet of water.

Some Tag Games

The excitement of tag games adds much to the fun of being in the water, and most of the games described here require little in the way of aquatic skill for enjoyment.

PLAIN TAG—One player is It, and the others in the game try to keep out of reach by swimming and diving into the water.

CROSS TAG—The one who is It points out his subject. The one selected must keep out of the way of It, for if he is touched he becomes It. If any player is caught between the man being chased and It, then that player becomes the one to be chased.

OSTRICH TAG—The participants are all bunched together at one end of the pool or in shallow water. The one named to be It must start chasing the others until he catches one. But to keep from being caught, a player can be safe by having one of his arms under one of his legs, and holding his nose with thumb and fingers. If he breaks this pose, he can be tagged, becomes It, and the game continues.

DING-DONG BELL—About a dozen players make this an exciting game. All except one are blindfolded with cloths which will not readily become undone. The one swimmer who can see goes into the water carrying a cowbell or similar small bell. At intervals he rings the bell and dives down into the water as he does so. The man with the bell is It until one of the blindfolded players catches him. Then the bell man takes the blindfold, and the one who caught him becomes the new It.

TOM, TOM PULL AWAY—All players except the one who is It line up on one side of the pool; It stands on the opposite side. The one who is It calls out "Tom, Tom," when everyone must plunge across the pool. Whoever is caught before reaching the other side helps catch others on the return plunge, and the game continues until all are caught. The game can be made more energetic by requiring that in order to be caught, a player must be pulled above the water if he is under the surface, or be ducked if caught on the surface, rather than merely being tagged.

BALL TAG—This can be a fast game, when played in a limited area. It can be played in waist-deep water for non-swimmers, in deep water for swimmers. Using a soft rubber ball, It tries to tag another player by hitting him with the ball. The one tagged becomes It. If It misses, the others may try to prevent him from recovering the ball.

JAPANESE TAG—The "emperor," a nonplayer, announces certain parts of the body which must be tagged by It; for example, "head," "right shoulder," "left hand," etc. Those who are tagged must join It and try to tag the remaining players. In another variety of this game, the "emperor" calls out certain parts of the body which must be out of the water to gain immunity from being tagged. It may tag any player not in the immune position. For example, the order may be "one foot out," "head under water, right hand out," "both feet out," etc.

LOG—This is an old, popular game which combines practice in floating with tag, and can be played with 5 or as many as 20 players. Spaces are marked off at opposite ends of the pool, or some objects in the vicinity may be designated as goals. The player who is the log floats on his back midway between the two goals. The other players swim in a circle around the log. Without any warning, the log suddenly rolls over and gives chase. The other players try to reach one of the goals without being caught. Any player caught must become a log and float in the center with the first log. The last one to be caught becomes log for the next game.

SIMON SAYS "HALT"—This is another game that can be played with 5 to 20 swimmers. The player who is It stands at the side of the pool outside of the water. He covers his eyes with his hands, and begins to count aloud from 1 to 10. As soon as he starts counting, all the other swimmers start to swim the length of the pool. After reaching 10 in his count, It says, "Simon says 'Halt'" and uncovers his eyes. When he does so, everyone must be motionless in the water. Anyone seen moving is sent back to the starting point. The game continues until all players swim the length of the pool, or give up.

TREAD-WATER TAG—One player is chosen to be It. The others swim about the pool. To escape from being tagged, a swimmer must be treading water when It reaches him. The tagger tries to touch a player before he can stop swimming and tread water. When a player is tagged, he changes places with It. A referee may be helpful in this game to determine whether a tag was made before or after the swimmer began treading.

HANDICAP TAG—This game can be played with as many as 15 players. The one who is It must try to tag the others as they swim about the pool. But he must tag them on the arm or leg. When a swimmer has been tagged, he continues to swim, but may not use the arm or leg which has been tagged. When he has been tagged several times and can no longer swim, he is out of the game. The swimmer keeping in motion longest wins.

HEAD TAG—This game is played in the water and alongside the pool. The player who is It must touch another on the head; that one in turn becomes It. Players may dive or jump in from the sides of the pool and may climb out to avoid It. However, no one is permitted to run around the *corners* of the pool. On reaching a corner, a player must jump or dive into the water. After It has tagged a player, he may not be tagged until another has been tagged and made It.

FISHTAIL TAG—The players are each given a piece of cloth about 3 feet long which is to be tucked into the backs of their swim suits or trunks at the waist. (Be sure to use color-fast cloth to prevent running.) These pieces are the fishtails which are the goals in this game. At the starting signal, each player will try to snatch as many fishtails as he can without losing his own. He may protect his fishtail by turning away from an opponent; he may not hold onto his own fishtail. The one who has gathered the most fishtails wins. In case of a tie, the tying individuals may be re-equipped with fishtails and battle individually for the title.

This may also be played as a team game, in which case the teams are each given fishtails with team colors. One point is given for each captured fishtail; two may be given for each fishtail that has survived the game in its wearer's trunks or swim suit.

Water Games for Beginning Swimmers

LEAPFROG—The players all line up in a straight line from the shallow end of the pool toward deeper water. Those on the deeper end may be treading water. The last in the line puts his hands on the shoulders of the one in front of him, pushing him under water, while he leaps over him with feet outspread. This continues with each player in turn until the one who was first in line becomes last. This game has been found a good way to make swimmers feel at home in the water.

THE FOX AND THE DUCKS—One player is selected as the Fox; another is chosen as the Mother Duck. Remaining players are Ducklings. The Ducklings form a line behind the Mother Duck, each one holding the waist of the one in front of him. The Fox, after the starting signal is given, attempts to catch the last Duckling in the line. The line, led by the Mother Duck, attempts to foil him by turning in various ways, but the line must remain unbroken. When the last Duckling is tagged, he becomes the Fox, and the Fox becomes the Mother Duck.

DODGE 'EM—An even number of players are divided into 2 teams. Team 1 forms a large circle around Team 2 at the shallow end of the pool. The team in the outside circle has two volley or water polo balls, with which they try to hit the players on the other team. Players inside the circle may walk, swim or duck under water to avoid being hit. When a player is hit with the ball, he must join the circle and help to hit the players still inside the circle. When all have been hit by the ball, the sides exchange positions and repeat, or the last two to be hit may be made captains and choose teams for the next round.

PIGEON—This is another old water game which is good for a mixed group of boys and girls—or adults. All the swimmers line up, sitting on the same side of the pool, with both hands clasped around their ankles and their chins on their knees. At the word "pigeon," all dive into the water, swim across the pool, and climb up on the other side, assuming the "pigeon" position. The last one to get into pigeon position is eliminated each time. The game continues until the last survivors are named "King Pigeon" and "Queen Piegon." For a faster game, the ends of the pool may be used, and the first ones to swim the length of the pool and assume the position may be the title holders.

Treading-Water Games

FISHERMAN'S CHOICE—One player is selected to be the Fisherman. He treads water in the center of the pool or playing area. All the other players are the Fish and line up at one side. At a signal from the Fisherman, the Fish must begin swimming across the pool. Those tagged by the Fisherman must stay in the center of the pool and help him catch the other Fish.

When the Fisherman has caught three Fish, the Fish who have been caught join hands, forming a "net" for the Fisherman in the center of the pool. Those on the ends of the net may tag. The ones in the center only try to prevent the Fish from breaking through. The Fish may swim under water, swim between those who form the net, or try to get around them. The last Fish to survive becomes the Fisherman for the next game.

TEN AND STOP—This is another game for 5 to 20 players. The leader stands facing the wall at one side of the pool. All the other players are lined up in the water at the opposite side of the pool. The leader counts slowly from 1 to 10, then says "stop," and turns around quickly. As he begins to count, the swimmers start toward him. When he says "stop," they stand if they are in shallow water, or tread water if they are in the deeper part of the pool. Any player whom the leader sees still swimming when he turns around is sent back to the starting place. The process is repeated until all players have reached the side on which the leader stands.

TREAD AND SPLASH—Two teams are lined up in the pool facing each other, about 6 feet apart. At the signal they begin to tread water and at the same time splash water with the palms of their hands toward the other line. The team that can stick it out the longest wins.

THE OLD WHISTLE GAME—This is one of the oldest water games, but it is still very popular. The group of swimmers is lined up in the pool, treading water. An ordinary whistle with a lanyard attached is thrown into the water. At the signal the players submerge and dive for the whistle. As soon as a player retrieves it, he comes up to the surface and tries to blow it three times. If he succeeds, he is the winner. Meanwhile, however, the other players are allowed to try to push him under the water so that he will not be able to blow the whistle or even cause him to drop it. A swimmer who comes to the surface without the whistle holds his hand over his head when he breaks water as a signal that he does not have the whistle and may not be ducked. Trying to pull the whistle out of a player's mouth is cause for disqualification.

Swimming Games

SWIMMING SPELL DOWN—The leader calls out a swimming stunt. Those who succeed in performing the stunt remain in the game; those who fail are eliminated, until only the champion is left. However, this game calls for some understanding on the part of the leader. Stunts should start with easy ones for the group at first, to prevent players from being eliminated too quickly, and they should gradually become more difficult.

POISON—A ring is formed in the pool by players, either holding hands or holding onto a rope circle. The "poison" is a floating object anchored in the center of the group. The object of the game is to maneuver so that others touch the poison. As they do they are eliminated and swim off. The last one left is the winner.

PRISON CAMP—This game is a "water" variety of a very old

Boy Scout game. The players, who may be of any convenient number, are divided into two teams who wear some identifying mark, such as similarly colored swim caps, armbands, etc.

Two prison camps are marked out on land at each end of the swimming area, and the water between them is considered neutral area. The object of the game is to capture as many of the "enemy" as possible by tagging them, and to free captured teammates.

When a member of one team captures an enemy, he escorts the captive to his team's prison camp where the prisoner must remain until the end of the game unless rescued.

Prisoners are rescued if a member of their team can manage to reach the camp in which they are held without being tagged. In some games all the prisoners are freed and may return to their forces unmolested; in others each prisoner must be tagged by a "free" member of his own team to be released. The game may continue until all the players on one side have been captured, or for some prearranged length of time. Without some time limit, this game may go on almost indefinitely.

Water Contests

Most of the "contests" described here are primarily of the type seen at camp waterfront exhibitions; but they may provide some ideas that could just as well be used in the family pool.

WALKING UNDER WATER—Four swimmers are necessary for this contest. Two, each carrying another on his shoulders, walk out from the shallow end of the pool toward the deep end, the object being to see who can stay down the longest.

TUG OF WAR—This contest has many variations and can be tried in either shallow or deep water. For the most impressive spectator show, the rope should be about 30 feet long, with hand loops for each swimmer, and about ten men to a team. Provide some marker at the starting point to show clearly when one team pulls the other across.

CANOE-TILTING CONTEST—This is one of the contest "stand-bys." Two participants are in each canoe, one to paddle, the other to do the jousting. Each fighter is equipped with a pole about 10 feet long, well padded at the ends. The paddlers maneuver the canoes and try to keep them from being overturned. The men with the poles try to push their opponents into the water. For variety, a number of canoes and "fighters" may be sent into the arena; the paddlers may or may not be allowed to take an active part in the battle.

BOXING ON A RAFT—For this contest, a raft should be built which is just about large enough to hold two contestants, if they balance a bit. The men on the raft are fitted with boxing gloves, and the object is to see which one can knock the other into the water. The "champ" may take on all comers.

LOG CONTESTS—A large, smooth log is a valuable adjunct to water contests. Two of the more popular "log" contests are burling and log walking.

In burling, two contestants sit on the log and try to unseat each other by rolling the log. More experienced "burlers" may try this while standing on the log, or they may be provided with long balancing sticks which they may use to help keep their balance and to overthrow their opponent.

In log walking, the object is to try to keep balanced on the log in an upright position. This is a contest against time, and a stop watch should be used to time the contestants and determine the winner.

PICKABACK WRESTLING—This is a popular beach game, but for water sport it should be played in water that is about up to the armpits of the "horses." Each player is part of a horse-and-rider team, the object being to unseat the other rider. The upper man locks his feet behind his "horse's" back, while the horse wraps his arms around the rider's shins. Both parts of the team are important. While the riders are trying to unhorse each other, the horses try to keep a firm balance by active footwork and judgment. In one variation of this game, the riders are blindfolded.

BUCKING BRONCO—For this game the players line up in pairs, with the bronco directly behind the rider. This rider stands with his feet wide apart. The bronco bends his knees and places his head between the legs of the rider. The bronco then straightens his body and carries the rider up on his shoulders. He next attempts to throw the rider backward into the water. The rider may not use his hands to remain on his "steed." Bronco and rider may then change places. With a small group, eliminations may enable the picking of a champion rider and a "killer" bronco.

Informal Races and Relays

Races and relays can add much to the enjoyment of water sport and can be used to inspire young toddlers to exert their best efforts, or to keep a gang of exuberant teen-agers busy. The wide variety of "stunt" races and relays will provide one to fit any group of swimmers—or nonswimmers —in almost any waterfront or pool situation.

CHARIOT RACE—The "chariot" can be a board, life preserver or buoyant cushion, drawn by 2 or 3 swimmers towing a "rider." To limit interference among the teams in a pool, the race could be run as a pursuit race, with the teams starting at opposite ends and swimming around until one laps the other. In a simpler form, the chariot race could consist of 2 or more swimmers, with arms interlocked about each other's shoulders, racing other teams.

CROCODILE RACE—The "crocodile" is formed by lining up two teams of equal numbers. Each man in the line locks his legs around the middle of the man behind him. The last man in each line uses only the kick for propulsion, the others use armstrokes. In another form, the teams line up with each man holding the one in front at the hips. Then, with the exception of the man in front, all use the leg kick to propel the team.

FLAG RACE—Even poorer swimmers can participate in the flag race or flag relay. Contestants swim on their sides or backs, holding the flags out of the water with one hand. Flags must not touch the water.

TUNNEL RACE—This is a good one for shallow water, working out best with from 8 to 20 persons divided into 2 teams. The members of the teams stand in line in shallow water or at the shallow end of the pool. The players, with the exception of the last one in line, stand with feet spread wide apart. At the starting signal, the last player in each line swims under water, between the knees of the other players, to the front of the line.

On reaching the front of the line, he stands and spreads his feet apart. The one who is then last in line watches carefully, and when the first swimmer's head appears above water, starts his underwater swim. When the race is finished the players will be lined up in the same order as at the start.

SCRAMBLE BALL—Provide about a dozen small corks or ping-pong balls. Divide the players into 2 equal teams and have them some distance apart at the start of the game. Throw the corks or balls into the water between the 2 teams. The object of the contest is for each team to get as many of the objects as possible for their "side." When all have been secured, blow the whistle to stop the round. Keep score of the number gathered by each side. The game continues until one side has secured the agreed upon number of objects for victory—25, 50, 100, etc.

EGG AND SPOON RACE—This has long been a summer camp favorite. Players start from a standing position with a spoon held in the mouth and an egg—or round stone of egg size—balanced on the spoon. The object is to swim the length of the course with the egg held on the spoon. If the egg drops off, it must be replaced before the swimmer may continue—or he may be required to return to the starting position. A similar race is the BALLOON RACE in which each contestant must propel a balloon the length of the course without using hands. The usual rules allow the use of feet, shoulders, head or any part of the body except the hands. Another variation is the BLOWING RACE in which a ping-pong ball is placed in front of each contestant, who must race the course keeping the ball in front of him by blowing on it. Touching the ball with the hands, propelling it by making waves, etc., disqualifies him.

RETRIEVING RACE—Obtain a dozen or so bright, sinkable objects that will be visible under water. Throw them into the water at random. The object is to see how many can be retrieved in one underwater try.

UMBRELLA RACE—Provide each entrant with an opened umbrella or parasol. The object is to swim the course, holding the umbrella upraised, without allowing it to touch the water.

Obstacle Swimming

Providing an obstacle may seem an unusual way to encourage poor swimmers, but the impediments in several of the obstacle swims described below will actually give some support to the novice swimmer, and better swimmers will enjoy the opportunity to overcome the handicaps imposed on them.

RESISTANCE SWIM—Swimmers pull boats or canoes containing a number of people. A swimmer may try to pull a canoeist paddling in the opposite direction, etc.

TOWEL RACE—Each contestant is provided with two large

Turkish towels. He must hold one in each hand—by a corner—while swimming the course.

CARRRYING THE BALL—Each player must carry a water polo or similar-sized ball between his knees while racing. A lost ball must be recovered, placed between the knees, and the race continued, or anyone losing his ball may be required to return to the starting point.

PADDLE RACE—Contestants must swim by paddling the body through the water with a regular-sized canoe paddle or small oar of the rubber lifeboat type.

OBSTACLE RACE—An obstacle course is set up in the water. It may be made up of boats or canoes, floats, logs, rubber tubes, etc. Swimmers must go over, under, around or through specific obstacles as instructed.

Drinking and Eating Under Water

These "amazing" stunts are not quite as difficult as they would seem, and the knack can be acquired by almost anyone who can keep his head under water for a short time.

DRINKING UNDER WATER—The only equipment needed is a bottle of soda pop, preferably a red beverage or one of some other bright color that can be seen by the spectators. The performer dives and comes up so that the neck of the bottle is under water and the rest is above the surface in plain view of the spectators. The secret is to hold the mouth over one side of the open end of the bottle and blow air up the side of the bottle. This will force the soda pop out of the bottle, but it appears to the spectators that the swimmer is drinking it.

EATING UNDER WATER—A small banana is the best "food" for this trick. Peel one end of the banana. Place the end in the mouth and keep pushing the rest of the banana against the mouth in such a way that the water cannot enter the mouth. Then flourish the empty banana peel before the audience.

Comedy Diving

Comedy dives are often the climax of indoor and outdoor swimming meets and water pageants. However, many of the truly effective comedy dives require little in the way of trained diving skill, and the youngster or teen-ager who can swim from the center of the pool to the side can participate in a comedy diving program and enjoy it. Rehearsals and the working out of the program are part of the participants' fun, and the family with an outdoor pool can encourage its children, and probably the neighbors', to provide an outdoor water circus that will be enjoyable for performers and audience alike.

In most instances the "build-up" and effectiveness of the performance of the "characters" can be increased by having an "announcer" who can personalize the show with references to local or family personalities.

"Take-off's" or impersonations of persons well known to the audience, or imitations of animals are usually good for a laugh. In most instances the bigger the "splash," the more pleased the audience is liable to be.

The clown divers who performed at the World's Fair and other professional shows had all the advantages of good equipment such as diving boards, diving towers, spotlights, and numerous colorful clown costumes, wigs, facial make-up, and professional training and natural diving ability.

However, the individual who possesses some gymnastic or acrobatic ability, who can perform a front, back, twisting, somersault or lay-out dive, who can pantomime with the "dead-pan" or other significant facial expressions, and who is not afraid to take a "beating" now and then will make the best clown diver.

Some young people make better "natural" diving clowns than others, and it appears to be a matter of personality rather than aquatic ability. Rolland Hill, director of safety services for the Newark, New Jersey, Chapter of the American Red Cross, who has done much work and research in this field of water activity, says, "I have seen many youngsters who were not particularly good swimmers, but had that daring 'show off' characteristic common to some more than to others. On several occasions groups of these young people were very easily talked into a game of 'Follow the Leader'—off a low diving board—which frequently included such simple clown dives as the 'rocking chair,' the 'statue,' the 'get acquainted,' the 'flying squirrel,' the 'cannon ball,' the 'neck,' the 'sitting bull,' etc. The game can readily be called a success when even the participants are laughing at themselves as well as at one another."

Comedy Dives

ROCKING CHAIR DIVE—Diver sits on end of board with legs hanging off end, rolls backward on board, bringing legs overhead and backwards until toes touch board, rolls forward and off board, entering water headfirst.

GET ACQUAINTED DIVE (a good dive for "Follow the Leader") —Regular approach, hurdle and spring. While in the air, keep pointing to self and shouting aloud your name: "I'm John Sylvester Jamieson." Entry is feetfirst. A variation could be a half twist after leaving board, so that other participants could see and hear you better.

STATUE DIVE—Diver makes regular approach, hurdle and spring, and while in the air assumes and holds a statue position: a shot-putter; a soldier saluting, etc. Made with feetfirst entry.

FLYING SQUIRREL DIVE—Regular approach and dive. While in the air, spread arms and legs. Tuck head just before entry.

CANNON BALL DIVE— (a) On take-off, strike a tuck position and hold. Enter water in sitting position. (Sometimes called a Pile Diver.) (b) A high-front dive. As body nears water, tuck body and do half of a front somersault. Enter water with a big splash.

NECK DIVE—Diver lies on back of board, with head just over end of board. Slowly raise legs straight over head until body is balanced on neck and shoulders. Pause. Then allow body to fall over straight, with feetfirst entry.

SITTING BULL DIVE—Take back-dive position on end of board. Bend forward. Keep legs straight, touch toes or grasp ankles. Hold position, lose balance, fall backward. Enter water in sitting position. (Better suited to a low board.)

WHIRLING DERVISH DIVE—Exaggerate approach and spring— full or half turn in air, hands over head on take-off, at sides for feetfirst entry. (Sometimes called a Spinning Top Dive.)

STANDING, SITTING DIVE—Take a standing position at end of board, facing forward, spring upward slightly, legs forward, spread sideward. Sit on board and rebound into a front dive. With some practice, clown divers have increased the difficulty of this dive to a Standing, Sitting, Standing Dive and also to a Standing, Sitting, ½ Twist to a Back Standing Dive. More advanced divers have also added front or back somersaults to the latter.

APE OR MONKEY DIVE—An imitation dive by a very hairy person who walks onto board with arms hanging down, knees bent, swaying from side to side. From deep squat or crouch at end of board, a headfirst entry with hands at sides.

BICYCLE DIVE—Run or spring off board, and while in the air "hold handle bars" and revolve legs quickly, as in riding a bicycle. (Sometimes called a Track Man or Runner's Dive, with arm movements included.)

CUPID'S DIVE—While in the air assume a "shooting arrow" position. If left arm is forward, bring left foot up and place on right knee. Keep right leg straight. Hold position through entry.

FOUNTAIN DIVE—Fill mouth with water before dive. Good,

high spring. While in the air, squirt water from mouth. Spread knees wide apart and place both hands on head for better effect. Feetfirst entry. (Sometimes called a Squirt Dive.)

APPLAUSE DIVE—High-spring dive. While in the air, clasp hands in front of body, behind the back, and overhead before the feetfirst entry.

CART-WHEEL DIVE—Start regular cart wheel (as on land) a few feet before end of board, so that body and legs come over and clear end of board for a feetfirst entry.

HANDSTAND DIVE—Grasp end of board or sides of board at end. Keep arms straight and kick up to handstand. Hold balanced position momentarily, then push off for headfirst entry, or duck head allowing legs and feet to drop over for feetfirst entry.

HANDSPRING DIVE—Performed in the same fashion as a handspring on land, with feetfirst entry. When learning, make rather slow approaches.

FALLING LEAF DIVE—A slow walking approach to about a half body length from end of board. Lean backward slightly, allow knees to bend forward, let knees sag to board, arch back and do a "chest roll" (turn face to one side), grasping sides of board with hands, so that enough push can be given to get body and legs around and over the head and off end of board. For persons not familiar with this common "acrobatic" stunt, it is suggested that they try it on soft ground, sand, or a tumbling mat several times before attempting it on the board.

FORWARD ROLL DIVE—Performed the same as on land, with roll being completed in a standing position on end of board, and following with any other dive off the end. A common variation is that in which the initial roll is completed in a squat and/or tuck position at end of board—a slight push, and continue the roll in same position. (The latter dive has also been called the Rolling Stone.)

HALF JACKKNIFE DIVE—Regular approach, hurdle, etc. Bend forward and grasp one leg at ankle with both hands. Hold this position throughout dive, including entry.

SIDE BOARD DIVE—Regular approach, and hurdle slightly to one side so that only one foot strikes board at end of hurdle. The other foot is well off to the side and below board. The body is well off balance and falls off board sideward.

"VERY HIGH" DIVE—Regular approach, a very high hurdle which takes the diver just beyond end of board during downward flight of body. At highest point of hurdle stiffen body and legs, hook feet, and descend in an awkward position for feetfirst entry. (Sometimes called the Missed Board Dive.)

SWAN SPLASH DIVE—One of the most common comedy dives, in which the diver executes a regular swan or front dive with head held back and body arched in flight. Entry, of course, is flat over on chest and stomach.

HALF-GAINER SPLASH DIVE—Actually the dive is completed with a splash in between a half and full gainer.

TOE OR HEEL DIVE—Hang by toes or heels from end of board momentarily before dropping into water. (Better suited to a high board.)

BANANA PEEL DIVE—Top surface of board or covering mat must be thoroughly wetted down to make it slippery. Make about a 2- or 3-step approach from back end of board, then slide the rest of the way on heel of one foot and toes and balls of other foot. This slide can be done right off end of board, or diver may stop the slide about a foot from end of board and make a complete twist turn or pirouette on the end before a casual or unconcerned "fall-off."

SWINGING CHANDELIER DIVE—Hang by hands at end of board, facing board. Start to swing body as on a horizontal bar. At high point of *backward* swing, let go and drop into a headfirst entry, or tuck body for a cannon-ball entry, or come around farther and straighten body for a back-splash entry. (Best done on a high board.)

BROKEN BACK JACKKNIFE DIVE—Starting position is same as for regular standing back jackknife dive. Take spring, but not as far backward or as high as in the regular dive. With arms straight, allow hands to come down on boards, legs spread apart. Push off board and allow body to fall into a back-splash entry with arms and legs extended toward ceiling or sky and chin tucked on chest.

JUMP ROPE DIVE—Hold a piece of rope long enough for jumping or skipping. Make a feminine skipping approach, holding an end of rope in each hand. Take a high hurdle and spring. Rotate or turn rope around body as many times as possible before entry.

BROKEN SPRING DIVE—Use regular approach and high hurdle (exaggerate arm-lifting motion). As soon as feet hit board, sink down to a deep knee bend or squat position, knees wide apart, and tip forward, hands in the "prayer" position. Make a grotesque, headfirst entry.

Partner Comedy Dives

Here again, as with the single or individual comedy dives, there are numerous clown antics which can be performed. Basically, of course, the variety and difficulty of such dives also depends on the skill and daring of the "characters." Following is a list and brief description of some of the more popular partner comedy dives or stunts:

LEAP FROG DIVE—One partner walks out to end of board, bends over to "size up" the situation. Second partner approaches low hurdle and does a straddle vault (hands on partner's back) over first partner.

OVER THE BACK DIVE—First partner makes a nervous, shaky, crawling (on hands and knees) approach to end of board. Touches top, sides, underside of board. Announcer asks what he is doing. Reply is, "All good divers have to get the feel of the board." In doing so, he remains on his hands and knees while second partner makes approach, springs and dives over him. Bouncing board causes first diver to fall off board.

BARGAIN BASEMENT—A good dive when "characters" are dressed as women and props include several cardboard boxes, etc. First partner starts approach, trips and falls on stomach as boxes are tossed into the air. Second "shopper" makes a fast walking approach (holding packages or boxes in such a way as to give the impression that his view is obstructed). He walks right over partner's back, off the board, and continues walking motion during downward flight.

WHEELBARROW DIVE—Partners assume same positions as for "Wheelbarrow" race on land, then move forward off end of board with rear partner keeping hold of "wheel's" ankles.

SIAMESE TWIN DIVE—Both partners stand side by side at back end of board, inside arms around each others waists. Both make the approach, hurdle, and dive in unison.

ROLLING SOMERSAULT DIVE—One partner lies on back, head toward rear of board, legs extended upward, hands grasping ankles of partner who straddles the "bottom" man. "Top" man starts a forward roll toward end of board, pulling bottom man up to a standing position, and so on until "top" man is able to make a front dive off board with "bottom" man following, still holding partner's ankles.

HORSE AND RIDER DIVE—One of the most common performed by clown divers.

The "rider" makes an approach, hurdle, and high vertical jump with legs spread wide apart. The "horse" has followed close behind and dives into a horizontal position between legs of "rider." The effectiveness of this dive can be greatly increased if the "rider" is able to perform a regular full gainer dive. If so, "rider" executes a very high full gainer (easier in tuck position and more difficult but more effective in lay-out position) and spreads legs wide apart as body starts downward. The "horse" has delayed his approach until the gainer is almost complete before he dives into horizontal position between legs of rider. Shout of "Hi, Ho, Silver," as they enter water completes dive.

ACROBAT DIVE—The comic possibilities of one acrobat trying to mount to a standing position on his partner's shoulders are well known to everyone who has seen circus gymnasts, vaudeville comic acrobats, or watched such performers on TV. Divers attempting this one should practice and work out details on land before trying it on end of board. General build-up routine usually includes the "slippery knee," "foot in pants" and "foot caught in rear." Once the top man is up and standing on partner's shoulders, possibilities are again numerous. Dive is often unexpectedly completed because of lack of balance.

TOP-PITCH DIVE—Another dive involving some gymnastic ability and preliminary practice on land. First partner takes a back-dive position on end of board with hands cupped in front of waist ready to catch a foot of second diver who approaches, places a foot in partner's cupped hands, and hands on partner's shoulders. Second man springs up off one leg as first man lifts and throws him over his head into water. (Sometimes called a Leg Throw Dive.)

ROPE DIVE—Requires a third "character" to "assist" or "judge" the contest between two clowns of about same size and weight. Two partners face each other standing sideways at end of board and holding a 3- to 5-foot length of rope between them. With toes on board and heels off side of board, each begins to lean backward (bodies held rigid) holding rope taut between them. They maintain balance and let out rope slowly, so that their bodies are leaning out a bit farther.

The contest is announced as a "tie" when third "character" quickly cuts rope with knife or sharp scissors which he kept concealed from contestants. Of course, when rope is cut, contestants both fall off sideward.

BACK HANDSPRING DIVE—First man lies on back (looking at partner) at end of board, knees flexed (bent upward) and feet on board. Second man approaches, placing hands on partner's knees. Partner catches shoulders in his hands. A slight push aids in forward momentum and carries second man around somersault or handspring over partner and off end of board for a feetfirst entry. Second man can try for a one-and-a-half somersault in the air, and may make it. Partners on board can follow almost immediately with "Neck Dive."

Safety in Comedy Dives

The safety factor should never be overlooked for any person who attempts to develop clown divers. Forgetting about safety in attempting to bring a diver along too rapidly would only expose the performer to unnecessary danger and possible serious injury. Conversely, the learner who sticks to fundamentals and the easier comedy dives until he has complete control in approaches, hurdles and body control in the air, will have less trouble when the time comes to try difficult dives. Logically, it is far better to have a diver learn how to do the various regular dives (front, back, twisting, somersault, gainer) first. In doing so, good approaches, hurdles, body control in air, and entries will have been mastered, and the clown antics in similar dives will come much easier.

The performance in a camp, public pool, or home pool show include only the comedy dives that are geared to the safe performance levels of the divers.

Chapter 10

COMPETITIVE DIVING

COMPETITIVE diving, technically called "spring-board" diving, is one of the most demanding of water sports. Diving meets are usually conducted under the rules of the Amateur Union of the United States and its various member associations, and are practically the same as the rules which govern Olympic competition. In formal meets, divers are required to perform 5 required dives: forward, back, reverse, inward, and front dive one-half twist; and 6 voluntary dives from among accepted competitive dives.

Each dive is scored on a rather complicated basis, with different dives being given different ratings according to a "difficulty ratings" table, and the diver being scored by his nearness to perfection in each of his 10 dives.

When judging a dive, only the dive is considered, without regard to the approach to the starting position. The points to be considered by the judges are: the run; the take-off; technique and grace of the dive during the passage through the air; entry into the water. Judges do not consider or score a diver's actions beneath the surface of the water.

Points for each dive are awarded on the basis of 10 to 0, according to the opinion of the judges, using a half-point scale, as follows:

Very Good	8½–10 points
Good	6½–8 points
Satisfactory	5–6 points
Deficient	2½–4½ points
Unsatisfactory	½–2 points
Completely failed	0 points

There is no short cut to skill in diving. Proficiency can come only after continual practice under competent instruction, and diving requires good physical condition and an innate sense of timing and balance. However, recreational diving as distinguished from competitive, can be enjoyed by almost every person with some degree of swimming ability, and even by those with just enough swimming ability to get from the center of the pool to the side.

Diving Safety

Every summer, newspapers report diving accidents and fatalities occurring during dives. However, experts in aquatic sports feel that practically all diving accidents can be avoided if the sport is approached with a modicum of common sense. Analysis of diving indicates that there are 3 points at which a diver faces the possibility of injury: 1) striking the board as he passes it; 2) impact on the surface of the water; 3) contact with the bottom of the pool or diving area.

If the diver keeps visually aware of the board tip, he can minimize the possibility of striking it with his body. Even in the hurdle, the tip can be observed with peripheral vision. Many beginners seem to make the mistake of looking straight ahead, which makes it difficult for them to be accurate in landing or balancing. Beginners should take their first board jumps under the supervision of a qualified instructor. A smooth, controlled walk on the board, with the weight carried quickly from heel to ball of foot should provide a proper take-off. Heavy pounding on the heels and lack of transfer of weight forward, jerkiness, distortion of body position, and speed variation in steps, are all practices which may result in the driver's striking the board. They may cause a too vertical rise or an actual cutback which brings the diver's body too close to the tip of the board.

Injuries from impact with the surface of the water are often the results of a diver's overestimating his ability. Divers should be restrained from using boards higher than the one-meter board until they are proficient at the low board. A shallow or flat entry from a low board may cause minor contusions, some physical discomfort and possibly loss of breath. From a higher board, injuries may be more severe—for example, broken blood vessels, black eyes and bloody noses, and possible vertebral injury.

Back, neck and shoulder injuries may result from the type of water entry in which one part of the body is stopped by the impact with the surface and the other continues in the direction of rotation. This may be caused by leaning too far forward on take-off, or lack of body tension in flight, and also by a strong effort to correct a dive which is going over by an overpull in the opposite direction.

Underwater recovery is important as a safety factor. The diver must hold his position, since relaxing tension too soon, rising to the surface before the momentum of the dive is spent, or landing on the bottom, may cause injuries similar to the strains imposed by an entry impact. An observer should watch the beginning diver's underwater position. Should his arms separate widely under water or drop beneath the body, the head is vulnerable to striking the bottom. The landing impact must be controlled by the arms and shoulders beneath the total body weight, or by the feet and legs in case of feetfirst entry.

In natural water diving, perhaps the most frequent cause of accident is unfamiliarity with the water depth or the

PROPER STANDING TAKE-OFFS AND WATER ENTRIES

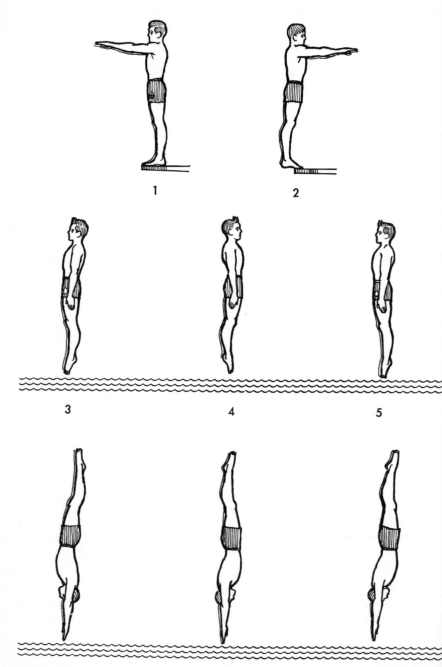

1. Starting position for all standing forward dives

2. Starting position for all back dives

3. Body and limb position for straight up and down entry—all reverse dives with body straight, or double reverse with tuck or pike, requiring this entry.

4. Proper position of head, arms and legs, on all back dives requiring feetfirst entry.

5. Proper position of head, arms and legs, on all forward dives calling for a feetfirst entry.

6. Proper position of head, arms and legs, for all back dives calling for a headfirst entry.

7. The straight up and down entry, correct when making inward dive or inward 1½ somersault.

8. Proper position of arms, head and legs on forward dives calling for a headfirst entry.

PROPER POSITIONS IN SPRINGBOARD OR PLATFORM DIVES

Proper form in forward 1½ somersault with pike—also when making inward dives calling for a pike execution

A proper tuck when making backward or reverse somersaults calling for a tuck execution

The proper position for a pike execution in backward dives—when making reverse somersault or 1½ reverse somersault (pike)

Correct position when making forward somersaults, doubles, or 2½ somersaults calling for a pike execution

Correct position when making front or inward dives with pike execution

Correct position for forward or inward somersaults calling for a tuck execution

(Courtesy A.A.U. Swimming Handbook)

existence of rocks and other dangerous debris at the bottom. A commonsense approach would rule out diving in unfamiliar water before the bottom has been carefully explored.

The Pressure Problem

Individuals differ widely in their tolerance of pressure on head, ears and sinuses. Anyone who may be sensitive to pressure should first try shallow dives to establish his tolerance level; and those with high sensitivity to pressure should not dive. Some people may be able to correct this condition by learning compensation breath control without actually blowing out. The use of earplugs, noseclips, etc. as "crutches" should be discouraged.

The possibility of accident may seem rather remote to the beginning diver. However, it is most important that proper diving habits be established from the start in take-off, balance, control in the air, entry and hitting bottom. As the diver continues, he dives with more height and cleaner entries and hits both surface and bottom with greater force, making proper techniques a must for his personal safety.

Execution of Dives

In competition, dives are judged on the following principles, which are taken from the regulations of the Amateur Athletic Union:

> The approach to the starting position is not taken into consideration; the starting position must be free and unaffected. The starting position in standing dives is assumed when the diver stands on the front end of the board, straight, head erect, feet together, with the arms straight and to the side or above the head. The forward approach must be smooth,

straight and forceful, and must comprise not less than three steps before the hurdle. The "hurdle" is the jump to the end of the board following the last step of the run when both feet must contact the end of the board simultaneously.

The take-off should be forceful, reasonably confident, and should proceed without undue delay. In running dives, the take-off from the springboard must be from both feet simultaneously immediately following the hurdle. A diver is entitled to his own method of arm swing on back take-offs, but must not lift his feet from the board before the take-off. When executing a backward dive, a diver must not bounce on the board or rock the board excessively before the take-off.

During the passage through the air, the body can be carried "straight," with a "pike," or with "tuck."

In the first case, the body must not be bent either at the knees or at the hips, the arms must be straight, the feet together and toes pointed.

With the pike, the body is bent at the hips, but the legs must be kept straight at the knees, toes pointed. The pike should be as compact as possible.

In the tuck, the whole body is bunched up with knees together, toes pointed. The tuck should be as compact as possible. The free position (a combination of layout, pike, or tuck) may be used in twisting dives only as listed in the AAU tables.

The position of the arms is at the choice of the diver, except in the case of the plain header forward (front dive), where the arms must be stretched out sideways in line with the shoulders during the flight through the air.

In dives with twists, the twisting must not be done directly from the board. In all pike dives with twists, the twist must not be started until there has been a marked pike position.

In somersaults with tuck (other than flying somersaults) the turn must commence as soon as the diver leaves the board, but in flying somersault dives there must be a well-defined header for approximately half a somersault, with the somersault made as rapidly as possible.

In dives with twists, the twisting must not be done directly from the board. In somersault dives with twist, the twist may be performed at any time during the dive at the option of the diver, unless otherwise specified.

Complete diving rules are available from the National Amateur Athletic Union, 3400 West 86th Street, Indianapolis, Indiana 46268.

Chapter 11

WATER POLO

THE present game of water polo and the various similar water games which preceded it came about as a result of the building of indoor swimming pools. Among the first of these were the "swimming baths" opened in 1820 in Paris which were restricted to use by women. Soon swimming pools were found in many places on the Continent and were growing more popular in England and Scotland. Efforts to relieve the monotony of swimming competition events led to the development of a water game which absorbed many of the elements of soccer and hockey.

Origins

In its first form, the game of "water soccer" was played at different pools under what would be considered "local" rules. In 1870, a committee of British swimming experts met to formalize rules for water soccer. After several years of confusion about the game, the Bournemouth Rowing Club staged what was probably the first formal water-polo match in 1876. With 7 members to a team, the game was played within a marked-off area under control of a referee and 2 goal judges. A goal was scored by placing the ball on a raft at the end of the playing area. However, contemporary reports indicate that this game was never completed, as the rubber ball which was used burst and brought all action to a halt.

The first set of recognized rules for the game of water polo were prepared by a Scotsman named Wilson in Glasgow in the late 1870's. By 1880, series of matches were being played among British and Scottish teams, although Wilson's rules received varying interpretations at different pools. Finally in 1885, the English Swimming Association officially recognized water polo as a separate branch of aquatic sport and ordered the universal acceptance of the rules which it adopted. The 1885 rules consisted of 11 points:

1. Duration of game—20 minutes.

2. Captains to agree or toss for choice of goals.

3. At start of play, referee throws ball into center of course. All players then enter water immediately except the 2 goalkeepers. Goalkeepers may remain out of water and defend goal as they think best.

4. Ball may be passed from one player to another, and carried either on or below the surface of the water to goal.

5. No player may interfere with goalkeeper either in or out of the water, or hold opponents in any way, unless goalkeeper or opponent is in possession of ball. In case of violation of this rule, a free throw is given to opposing team from place where foul occurred.

6. A goal is obtained by ball being taken up by hand and placed fairly on floating stage or boat provided for that purpose.

7. If ball goes "offside" during play, the referee must immediately return it to play; if it goes out over or on floating stage or boat, it must immediately be taken up and thrown into play by goalkeeper on the stage or boat.

8. Umpires, or one of them, shall blow whistle immediately after a goal has been scored, and play shall stop at that moment.

9. Teams shall change goals at half time.

10. Any competitor who withdraws from a match or fails to participate in a match for which he has been engaged, forfeits all prizes he may have already won at this meeting, as well as any he may afterwards become entitled to in connection with the same match.

11. Power is given to umpires, or in case of their disagreement to referee, to decide all circumstances not provided for by these rules.

Changes in the Game

During the decade of the 1890's, the game of water polo spread widely. Irish teams joined the British and Scottish teams. In America the rules were changed to make the game more practical in smaller, covered pools. In the American game the goal was scored by touching a mark painted on the wall, not by throwing for a goal. Water polo also spread to Germany, Austria and Hungary, where international competition was held. It also became popular in Australia, and soon spread to Russia.

During the 1950's, changes in the rules made the game faster and more colorful by eliminating the many stops and actionless periods caused by the old rules. In 1950, the International Water Polo Board, the recognized rule-drafting organization, adopted what are basically today's rules for the game.

Modern Rules

The modern game of water polo, which adopted many of the innovations introduced in the United States' form of the game, is played in a pool—or pool area—not more than 20 feet in width, and not less than 19 yards long. At either end of the playing area, goals 3 feet high and 10 feet wide, backed with netting, are set at water level. The teams are made up of seven members on each side, one of whom is the goalkeeper. Team members are identified by the colors of their bathing caps and by numerals on the caps identifying the players and their positions on the team; goalkeeper, leftback, rightback, halfback, left forward, center forward and right forward.

In the formal game, called "hard-ball" water polo, an inflated ball 27 inches in circumference is used. The ball is tossed into the center of the playing area, and contestants fight for possession of it. The ball may be advanced toward the goal by batting it with the body, "dribbling," or by balancing it in one hand. The object of the game is to score goals by hitting the ball through the net defended by the opposing side, using the head, feet or hands. At least 2 players must touch a ball before a goal may be scored.

The game is divided into 4 5-minute periods. Fouls such as carrying the ball under water or with two hands, tackling, bumping, etc. are called by a referee from outside the pool, and the penalty is an award of free throws to the opposing team.

Softball Water Polo

In American collegiate circles and among some water-sports clubs, the softball form of water polo has become popular—although many foreign critics of this particular game describe it as underwater mayhem. In the softball variety the goals are smaller, a much smaller ball is used, and the ball is flexible enough to be grasped by the fingers. All types of rough play are permitted, with choking, butting, tackling and holding opponents under the water all being acceptable tactics.

In the United States water polo has never become a widely popular participant sport. One limiting factor is that it is a game in which only expert swimmers take an interest, and it is a tiring activity, even for good swimmers who are not in top physical condition. It is most popular among those who have passed the peak of their competitive swimming careers, yet who wish to participate in an active water sport. Probably for this reason, and because play in the game is intricate and difficult, most championship teams include men who are from 35 to 40 years old.

Another factor that has limited the spread of water polo is that in most places playing facilities are inadequate. The standard outdoor water-polo court is about 20 yards by 30 yards, and indoors the rules call for an area of 20 feet and 19 yards. Many pools are not large enough to provide the proper playing area, and to have 14 swimmers competing for the ball in limited space is not conducive to good play. In addition, many pools large enough for the sport have a shallow end, which spoils the game.

Water Polo Competition

While a number of schools and colleges engage in water-polo matches, the Olympic competition and the national championships recognized by the American Athletic Union have been dominated by the athletic clubs. The New York Athletic Club and the Illinois Athletic Club have been among the top teams since the early 1900's. In the past few years, the sport has been spreading on the West Coast. With general acceptance of the "hard ball" and closer supervision of games by officials, the sport is expected to grow in popularity among players and spectators.

The official rules of water-polo competition may be found in the *Official Swimming Handbook* of the Amateur Athletic Union of the United States available from the A.A.U., 233 Broadway, New York 7, New York, for $1.50.

Playing Technique

In European methods of training for water polo, a sharp distinction is made between the type of swimming used in competition and in water polo. The progress of a competitive swimmer in the water is continuous, with emphasis on speed and endurance for longer events. The water-polo

This is a relatively calm moment in a water-polo game, with competing players both above water and concentrating on the ball.

player's swimming is varied in intensity and interrupted by the progress of the plays in the game. Also, the game calls for the player to hold his head high, in order to follow the progress of the ball and the game. In addition, the competitive swimmer need perfect only one stroke, while the competent water-polo player must be equally skilled in all the strokes and techniques he may need during the same. The "purists" of the sport decry the practice of many coaches of selecting aspirants who prove limited in competitive skill to form a water-polo team for a club or school.

The strokes necessary in water polo are the crawl, sidestroke, breaststroke and backstroke, although the various strokes must be adapted to the specific needs of the player during a game.

The Crawl

The crawl stroke is used during the greater part of the game, for it is the stroke used by a player in changing his position within the playing area. Since the swimmer must keep his head high to observe the game and the other players, his head must be held up. With the head held up, the legs will sink deeper than in competitive swimming. This changes the position of the body in the water. The higher angle of the body makes the legstroke more difficult. To compensate for this, the legs must be bent more at the knees to bring the feet nearer to the surface.

The armstroke must also be adapted to the needs of the game. In order to give support to the raised head and shoulders, the recovery stroke must be shortened. This is done by bending the elbows slightly so that the hands reach the water more quickly, producing a more forceful armstroke. Swimming with the arms slightly bent is also necessary when dribbling the ball along the surface of the water.

The Sidestroke

For maneuverability during plays and for quick turns, the sidestroke is important in water polo. However, this stroke as used in water polo differs from the competitive sidestroke. It is a modified sidestroke with emphasis on the powerful scissors kick. The armstroke is also changed, with the elbow of the arm moving in the air being sharply bent, giving an accelerated armstroke. The body is turned high on its side, with the eyes looking to the side. The legs are submerged just enough to provide support for the scissors kick. This half-side body position changes when one of the arms swings forward during recovery. Then the body is turned on the chest so that the raised head looks ahead. With the body in this position, the player sinks the arm that is swung forward into the water, and a forceful pull occurs simultaneously with the closing of the legs, pushing the body forward. When the pull begins, the body is turned again on the side to reduce water resistance. During the pull, the other arm reaches forward under the water, so that when one arm, completing the pull, swings back into the air, the other arm provides a continuous glide with an oarlike motion toward the breast.

The player should develop facility in using the sidestroke on both sides to meet the needs of the game.

The Breaststroke

During much of the action in a game, the player must rise high out of the water as in throwing or receiving passes, shooting goals, attempting interceptions. The goalkeeper must especially be ready to "jump" out of the water to defend his goal. For these situations, the breaststroke is advocated. Again, the stroke differs from its namesake used in competitive swimming. Here, emphasis is on the upward effect of the kick, and not on the forward propulsion of the stroke. The normal breaststroke calls for an almost flat position in the water. The water-polo player using the breaststroke forms an angle of 40 to 60 degrees with the surface. The pull which provides forward momentum is reduced to a bare minimum, and the press, which lifts the upper potrion of the body, is increased to the maximum.

The Backstroke

The backstroke is a "sometime thing" in water polo. It is used mainly when a player, swimming rapidly wants to observe the action of the game. While swimming the crawl, he simply turns over and continues swimming backstroke without losing his forward speed.

Proponents of the "scientific" approach to water polo say that while this stroke may not be used very often, it should be practiced with emphasis on holding the head up. As an exercise, using the backstroke is said to develop all-around mobility in the water, and it utilizes groups of muscles which are used less in other swimming strokes although they are used in play during the game.

Treading Water

Treading water is the technique of keeping the body in a vertical position in the water and is a useful resting and starting position. With the body held vertically, the legs perform a motion which is a combination of the leg movements used in breaststroke and sidestroke. The legs in treading do not move together, but successively, which gives this exercise its name. By closing the legs together quickly, the player can rise high out of the water. While treading, the hands perform a fanlike motion close to the hips. In rising out of the water, the hands can help by exerting a downward pressure. While treading water, the player can practice holding and passing the ball, using one and both hands.

Dribbling

Dribbling—changing of position with the ball—is among the most important maneuvers in water polo. It is used in escaping from an opponent, in getting into scoring position, in moving the ball around in the field of play. The technique of moving the 27-inch-circumference ball around is based on the crawl stroke described earlier in this chapter. To hold possession of the ball, even when moving at top speed, the player's body must be kept high in the water and his head and upper body well above the surface.

The objective in dribbling is to move the ball along about 4 to 8 inches in front of the head, on top of the wave created by the raised head and chest. With the proper water-polo crawl, the arms are bent inward at the elbow, speeding up the recovery portion of the stroke. Also, should the ball slide to the side, it may be controlled by the bent arms; the arms come alongside the ball at shorter intervals, and when necessary the ball may be grasped quickly.

Team Play

In many water-polo games, even in international and Olympic competition, the object of the game appears to be to get the player with the ball and hold him under water until loss of breath requires him to relinquish it, also to "dunk" an opponent frequently and for long enough periods, to impair his playing efficiency. Wrestling, holding, and other underwater forms of mayhem, are considered acceptable in many water-polo circles as long as they are not observable by the officials above the surface of the water.

In the early stages of water polo, the ball was thrown from one goal toward the other with no specific plan. Every player would swim toward the spot where the ball landed and strive for possession. Passing was done with rigidly outstretched arms, which made control difficult. In the modern "scientific" game, it was found that instead of long and random throws it was more effective to swim with the ball toward the opponent's goal and "'shoot" for goals from shorter distances. Swimming with the ball, dribbling, and improved ball handling led to team techniques resembling those of basketball, with the ball often being passed to a swimming teammate and more "air" play of the ball.

Chapter 12

OTHER WATER GAMES

WHILE water polo calls for expert swimming and physical stamina, there are other aquatic games which can be enjoyed—as participants—by poor swimmers and even nonswimmers, and they are also fun to watch. Many variations of these games can be played and all sorts of rules added or modified, according to the wishes of the players. Rules, once established before the game, should be strictly adhered to, and a referee should be appointed for the sake of safety and harmony among the players. The games may be varied by applying rules from hockey, water polo, or basketball.

Marine Ball

This game was designed for playing in the large shallow area of a public pool.

PLAYING AREA: 40 yards by 20 yards. Water should not be more than 3 feet deep.

EQUIPMENT: (1) Cork float boundary line (number of lines depending on shape of pool). (2) One 8-inch rubber ball. (3) Set of lacrosse or hockey nets—or any makeshift setup which serves the same purpose. (4) One set of bathing caps of the same color, choice of color to go to team winning toss.

RULES: (1) Nets—To be placed directly opposite each other at each end of playing area, if possible on wall of pool.

(2) Number of players—Between 7 and 12 on a side, depending on size of shallow area.

(3) Players' formation— (a) Goal tender or guard, directly in front of net; (b) at least 2 guards stationed right and left, 10 feet to either side of goal; (c) a center; (d) remainder of team are forward.

(4) Defense—Two methods of defense may be used, as in basketball, "man for man" and "zone." If teams are picked according to age or weight, "man for man" is best defense to use. This is a passing game, but tackling with no punishing holds is allowed. Swimming ability does not play too much of a part in performance.

(5) Start and ball in play—Ball is tossed into the air from side of pool by referee, between two players who scrimmage for possession. Ball is passed to forwards who work it down to scoring position, passing as in water polo, but a player may touch ball with both hands. Only a player in possession of ball may be tackled, and never by more than one man. Referee to decide on rough tactics or foul play.

(6) Scoring— (a) Ball must be thrown into net. (b) Goal to count 2 points. (c) If referee calls a foul, person fouled gets a free throw 15 feet from goal—this will count one point. (d) Ball is put back into play by referee who tosses ball to a guard of team scored against.

Double Water Ball

This game was originated and copyrighted by Nathan H. Kaufman of Pittsburgh, Pennsylvania, in 1933. He reports that it is now being played all over the world and "it is the only game ever invented that is completely original for swimming since it is almost impossible to play on land."

The game of double water ball may be played in shallow as well as deep water. Two balls are used, each side controlling one ball at start of game. Object of the game is to protect your own ball from the opposite team while trying to secure their ball also. Zones should be 5 feet away from each wall inside pool. Balls used are rubber, about 7 inches in diameter. Each team may consist of from 4 to 10 players.

In case of a foul, offender is immediately disqualified and cannot return to game until a score has been made. Fouls include: rough play, ducking an opponent who does not have the ball (other ball must be secured by teammates and passed to ball carrier in order to score), intentionally throwing ball out of pool, hitting an opponent with ball, etc.

Full game consists of 3 periods of 4 minutes each. Captain must throw ball out of zone to a member of his team. Ball is passed around and kept away from opposing team by defenders. Attackers attempt to secure ball from other team.

When both balls are in possession of any one member of team, it shall count one point if balls are touched together. When played in deep water, a point cannot be scored if ball carrier holds onto ball.

Water Skim Ball

This game may be played either width or length of pool, depending on age and skill of players. Purpose of game is to secure ball from other team when thrown in by referee, and after passing it around, attempt to score a goal by "skimming" or bouncing ball on water so that it will strike goal or go through it, after bouncing on water once. Zones are 5 feet away from each wall on inside of pool. A solid goal or framework may be used; it should be 2 feet high and 4 feet wide. Balls used are 7-inch and of rubber; teams consist of from 4 to 10 players.

The goal watcher is the only one allowed to protect his goal and must pass ball out of his zone in 10 seconds or forfeit it to other side. Goal watcher cannot score unless he swims out of his own section.

The game is made up of 8-minute halves. Teams line up in water, holding wall with one hand, in their own zones. No one is allowed to cross opposite zone line at any time during game. If ball, after skimming off water, hits anyone on opposite side and then strikes goal, it counts as a goal scored. Goals score 2 points; fouls score one point. Ball must be thrown with one hand and must be handled by more than 2 players before score can be made. Anyone holding ball may be ducked until it is released. An awarded foul throw must be made at an unguarded goal, from halfway between both goals, and must skim water and strike or go through goal to count. Fouls consist of holding onto wall with ball, rough play, stopping ball while holding onto wall, ducking player who does not have ball, etc.

Water Box Ball

This game is played the width of pool in shallow water 3 to 4 feet in depth. The ball is made of rubber and about 7 inches in diameter. The goals—from which game gets its name—are 2 boxes facing playing area, one on each side of pool, and 3 feet back from edge. They should be about 5 feet up on a support or platform. Boxes should be a foot high, a foot deep, and about 2 feet wide. Open tops of the boxes face each other, and word GOAL may be painted inside.

Five-feet throw lines are marked parallel to sides of pool. Three or more players make up a team. The game consists of 2 halves of 7 minutes each. Object of game is to toss ball into goal. Ball must be thrown with both hands, and to be counted a fair score must hit in the back of box. Ball must be tossed from outside 5-foot throw line. Each goal counts one point.

Game is started by both teams lining up in the water at respective sides of the pool, holding the wall with one hand. The ball is thrown into center of playing area by referee at beginning of game, and after a goal is scored. No fouls are called, but any player guilty of rough play or other offense may be taken out of game.

Rules on tackling, ducking, holding, etc., should be agreed upon by players before game is started.

Uno-Goal Polo

This game proved highly popular when tried by the Department of Recreation and Parks in Los Angeles. Basically, it is a combination of basketball and water polo, and is a good game for fairly expert swimmers looking for a lead-up game before trying water polo.

A regulation water-polo ball is used in an area about 15 to 20 yards square, with water at least 3 feet deep. The goal is an inflated automobile inner tube. If possible, any old-style tube with as large a radius as possible should be used—a truck tube is ideal. Around goal there is an "imaginary" penalty area of 3 yards.

Teams consist of 5 players and 3 substitutes. Goal tender is the only player allowed to enter penalty area or touch goal.

Playing time is 20 minutes, divided into 4 5-minute quarters, with one minute between quarters and 5 minutes between halves.

At start of game, each team places one man in each corner of square playing area. Goal tenders face each other directly in front of referee who blows his whistle to signal the start and throws ball between them. Once the game is on, players may enter any part of playing area except penalty area around goal.

A goal, worth 2 points, is scored when ball is thrown inside tube. No goals may be scored by goal tenders. If tie occurs at end of game, a 3-minute overtime is played. If score is still tied after overtime has been played, the first team to score a goal wins.

Following each goal, ball is dead and must be put back

into play by opposing goal tender, who passes it. If ball lands within 3-yard penalty area, it must be retrieved by a goal tender who passes it out to a teammate. If ball is thrown out of playing area, referee tosses it to nearest opponent from where it left playing area.

Scored fouls count one point. An ordinary foul is called against the goal tender if he moves more than 3 yards from goal, or if he moves goal out of place as a ball is thrown toward it. Ordinary fouls are called against all players if they stand or touch bottom during deep-water play; hold ball for more than 10 seconds; hold it under water or strike it with clenched first; start play before starting whistle; delay game; hold or duck an opponent.

Penalty for an ordinary foul is a free throw to goal from place where foul occurred, taken by player from opposing team nearest the offender. All other players stay in position until ball has left his hands.

Penalty for a "willful" foul is a free throw, as for an ordinary foul, and offender is removed from water, without substitution, until a goal has been scored. Willful fouls include: an ordinary foul committed deliberately; wasting time; any player except goal tender entering 3-yard area; changing position during a foul throw; goal tender interfering with a free throw; leaving field of play without permission of referee; refusing obedience to referee.

A free throw which rebounds from goal remains in play.

Water Basketball

This game may be played in a pool or in shallow water. Two hoops, peach or bushel baskets, or basketball baskets, are suspended 5 feet above water, facing each other at sides of pool, or about 40 feet apart. Generally, rules of basketball apply, except that players may advance while holding ball. Tackling and ducking are considered fouls and are punished by an award of a free throw at basket from distance of 15 feet.

Usually there are no out-of-bounds rules and a basket may be thrown from anywhere in the water. A basket counts 2 points and a score foul one point. It has been found that the game is less tiring if played in water not more than waist deep. An excellent game for poor or nonswimmers if played in shallow water.

Water Baseball

This game may be played in a pool, or at a beach or lake. In open water, the "diamond" is marked off by "bases" which may be stakes, or securely anchored buoys. Life preservers or seat cushions may be used for buoyed bases. In a pool, points at edge may be marked as bases; there is no need for a pitcher's plate, as no pitcher is used.

Batter knocks ball into playing "field" as he would serve a volley ball, then swims toward first base. In pool play, batter usually stands on edge of pool, serves ball, then dives into water and heads for first base.

Usual rules of baseball apply from then on, except that "catcher" serves as a fourth baseman, guarding home plate. Size of playing field can vary according to age and skill of players; number of players involved can be very flexible.

Water Volley Ball

Teams in this game can depend on available supply of participants. Players are divided into 2 teams, and a strip in center of playing area may be marked off as a neutral zone—corresponding to net in on-land volley ball.

If net is used, hang so that bottom is about 3 feet above water. A water-polo ball may be used; players bat it back and forth over net or neutral zone, using hands. A side loses ball if it fails to return it, if it hits net or falls in neutral zone, or if it is batted over limit lines.

If serving side wins ball, it scores one point. Only serving side scores. If it loses ball, it fails to score. Game is usually played until one side scores 21 points. In pool game, teams usually rotate from deep to shallow side.

Water Punch Ball

This game calls for a bit of equipment and some construction work, but where it has been used, results seem to justify the extra effort. A heavy, taut wire is stretched about 9 feet above surface of water of pool, running length of pool down the middle. Suspended from this cable on a sliding brass ring is a standard punching bag, at the end of a 7-foot rope.

Group of players is divided into 2 teams, each remaining on its side of the wire. A rope floating with wooden beads may be run on water underneath supporting wire to make team limits. Each team is given one end of pool as its goal, and object of game is to bat punching bag to that end while opposing team is trying to reach other end with bag. The game received its name because the pool in the ensuing melee looks like a veritable punch bowl. Rules may be set up to provide for rotation from deep to shallow end of pool and to limit physical contact.

Break the Balloon

Younger children will enjoy this game, which may be played at either deep or shallow end of pool, depending on water skill of participants. Necessary equipment is a supply of toy balloons.

Divide players into 2 equal groups, letting them choose sides, or selecting them by age or size. One team surrounds a balloon floating on water. At a signal, team of attackers tries to break balloon, while defending team protects it.

Each team can be given 2- or 3-minute attacking periods. Team which breaks balloon in shortest time, or side which breaks most balloons, wins. Referee should have a shrill whistle with which to signal a halt when play becomes over-enthusiastic, as younger players may forget objective in heat of competition and try to eliminate competitors.

Chapter 13

SWIMMING

THE ability to support oneself on the surface of the water and self-propulsion through the water without artificial aid are the basic requirements for participation in any aquatic sports. Swimming itself is generally considered one of the finest sports for developing and keeping muscular tone. It probably calls more muscles into play, with close co-ordination, than almost any other activity. The objective in proper swimming is to accomplish passage through the water with the least possible resistance to the ambient medium, with a minimum of splashing, and a smooth, continuous forward motion.

The Crawl

The "speed" stroke in most common use today is the Australian crawl which was developed in that country and improved in the United States. In the crawl the body is prone. Alternating overarm strokes and a flutter kick are used, and the head is turned from side to side at water level for breathing. While this is the stroke usually used in free-style racing, it is best used by untrained swimmers only for short distances, as it can be rather tiring after a short spurt of speed. The popular 6-beat crawl is accomplished by kicking 3 times while each arm is pulling. The breathing must be synchronized with the arm and leg motions. The head should be carried so that the waterline is just above the eyes. As the arm is extended forward, the head is turned to the opposite side, and the swimmer inhales, breathing quickly through the mouth. As the face is turned downward, exhalation is through the nose and mouth while the other arm is extended and pulling.

The Trudgen Stroke

For distance swimming, the trudgen stroke is considered less tiring than the crawl and is essentially a fast stroke. It is named after John Trudgen, a British swimmer who died in 1902. Trudgen gained international fame for his swimming victories using this stroke. It became popular first in Spain, then spread to Latin America and finally to the United States. This stroke combines the arm motions of the crawl and the leg action of the sidestroke—a modified scissors kick. Overarm strokes from a prone position are used, and the head remains on one side, for more natural breathing than in the crawl.

The important arm action of the trudgen is as follows: The stroke is started by pressing the arms alternately through the water with elbows straight. This motion is carried through until the elbow reaches the surface of the water close to the body. The elbow should then be lifted from the water until the hand emerges, and the hand is extended just above the surface until the arm is straight. When the hand enters the water, the arm should be pressed straight down for another stroke. As one arm presses through the water, the other reaches forward toward the start of the stroke.

For the leg motion, one hip is kept about 4 inches lower than the other as the scissors kick is started. The body motion is a forward roll through the water. Co-ordination of arms and legs is important. The leg motion must be geared to the position of the hips. With the *left* hip low, the kick is performed as the left hand moves forward; then the legs are kept together as the right hand goes forward. With the right hip low, the reverse action is followed.

There are several variations on the basic trudgen stroke. The use of a frog kick will reduce the amount of body roll. The "double trudgen" is accomplished by using a frog or scissors kick with each armstroke. The "trudgen crawl" is a form of the stroke in which a scissors kick is used while one arm is pressing, and 2 or 4 crawl-stroke kicks are used while the other arm is pressing.

The Sidestroke

The sidestroke is a relaxing swimming technique, probably best for long-distance swims and for rescue work. As the name implies, the swimmer lies in the water on whichever side is more natural and comfortable. With one ear in the water, he extends his underarm ahead of him along the surface of the water, and the upper arm alongside the top leg. At the beginning of the stroke, the reaching hand is cupped slightly and swept down to the front of the breast. At this point it meets the other hand which meanwhile has been slowly brought up in front of the chest, the hand moving edgewise to reduce water friction. At the meeting position, the force of the pull is transferred to the other cupped hand, which pushes down along the body to the top of the upper thigh. As this motion is being performed, the lower hand is returning to its extended position. The position of the "start" is held during the glide portion of each stroke.

The leg action, a scissors kick, is started with the feet together. They are moved toward the hips. When they are up as far as they can come comfortably, the feet are separated, the top leg moving forward, the lower leg backward. After the legs are separated as far as possible, they are snapped

BACKSTROKE

BREASTSTROKE

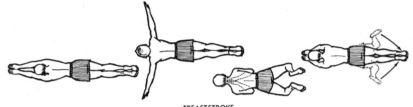

SIDESTROKE

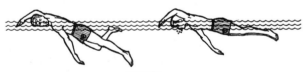

TRUDGEN

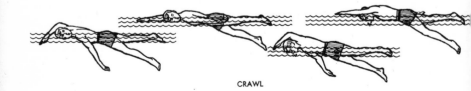

CRAWL

together from this spread position in one continuous motion —in effect as if a pair of scissors was being closed.

Breathing is usually effected by inhaling as the legs come together and exhaling as they separate.

The Breaststroke

This is another valuable long-distance stroke. In it, both hands must be pushed forward together from the breast, on or under the surface of the water, and brought backward simultaneously and symmetrically. The body should be kept perfectly on the breast and both shoulders in line with the surface of the water. The feet should be drawn up together, knees bent and open. The movement is a continued rounded and upward sweep of the feet, bringing the legs together. In competition, up and down movements of the legs in the vertical plane are prohibited. One part of the head should always break the surface of the water.

There are 2 forms of leg action which may be utilized in the breaststroke—the whip kick and the frog kick.

In the whip kick, the stroke starts with the legs fully extended. Then the heels are drawn up toward the hips, and the knees separated just about the width of the hips. When the knees are drawn up just below the hips, the feet are turned outward, toes toward the knees, and are moved to the side until they are separated beyond the width of the hips. In a continuing motion, the feet are pressed back and down, making a circle, until the feet return to the starting position.

The frog kick starts with legs extended and feet together. Then the feet are drawn toward the body, knees spread. The legs are extended until they are in line with the thighs, and are then snapped together with a motion originating at the hips. The action of the knees and feet must always be on a level plane, with no up and down motion.

The arm action starts with arms extended overhead, palms

down, and hands together. Palms are pressed outward and back slightly down until the hands are in line with the shoulders. Elbows are brought to the side, and the forearms and hands under the chest and neck. In a continuous motion, the hands are extended forward beneath the surface to the starting position.

The face may be kept up at all times in this stroke, or if it is submerged on each stroke slightly, one should inhale as the head comes up when the hands are pressing down and back.

The Butterfly Stroke

The butterfly stroke is seen most often in competition, being one of the required strokes in Olympic events. In the butterfly stroke, both arms must be brought forward together over the water and brought backward simultaneously and symmetrically. The body must be kept perfectly on the breast, and both shoulders in line with the surface of the water. All movements of the feet must be executed in a simultaneous manner. Simultaneous up and down movements of the legs and feet in the vertical plane are permitted. When touching at the turn, or on finishing a race, the touch must be made with both hands simultaneously on the same level with the shoulders, in the horizontal position. Any sidestroke movement disqualifies a contestant. When a swimmer is in the underwater position at the start, when turning or during the race, he may be allowed to make one or more leg kicks.

The Backstroke

For distance swimming, the backstroke combines alternate frog kicks and strokes of the arms, extended at shoulder level and moving in an arc toward the hips. The back crawl or racing backstroke offers the advantage of speed and a face-up position for visibility.

The starting position is on the back, with the body in a sort of sitting position with arms overhead about 4 inches from the ears. The legs should be straight and almost together, toes pointed. The head should be inclined toward the chest.

For the arm pull, the palm of the hand should be turned outward for the catch, and the straight arm then pushed toward the feet and drawn to the side of the body. The stroke should not be too deep in the water, perhaps about 6 to 14 inches beneath the surface, and the pressure should be even all the way through the arm pull. When the stroke is completed, the wrist should be in a position which allows a final backward push as the hand is drawn toward the thigh. As one arm completes the motion, the other starts its stroke. The arm should be relaxed on the above-water recovery, with little finger outward and palm down toward the surface of the water.

In the leg action, the kick is from the hips with an upward and out flip of the instep, giving a kick of slightly over 12 inches. The ankles should be held loosely and the toes pointed inward. The knees should be flexed to allow the instep to lash upward and backward during the force portion of the kick. In timing, the leg kick should be 3 to each armstroke, or 6 kicks for the full armstroke cycle.

The Olympic and Amateur Athletic Union rules for backstroke in competition state:

> The competitors shall line up in the water, facing the starting end, with the hands resting on the end or rail of the bath (pool) or starting grips. The feet, including the toes, shall be under the surface of the water. Standing in the gutters is prohibited.
>
> At the signal for starting and when turning they shall push off and swim upon their backs throughout the race. The hands resting on the end or rail of the bath must not be lifted before the signal of starting.

Any competitor leaving the normal position on the back before the foremost hand has touched the end of the course for the purpose of finishing shall be disqualified.

A competitor in a backstroke event must not turn over beyond the vertical toward the breast before the foremost hand has touched the end of the pool or course for the purpose of turning. A competitor violating this regulation shall be disqualified.

The Dog Paddle

While not honored with recognition as accepted stroke, the dog paddle is an excellent first start for many swimmers. This stroke, given its name because of its resemblance to the way a dog swims, is performed by reaching forward with the arms under water while using a modified flutter kick.

Olympic Swimming

In the late nineteenth century, swimming became recognized as amateur sport in many countries. With the development and improvement of swimming pools its popularity increased, and in the first modern Olympic Games held in Athens in 1896, swimming events were included as a major competition. In 1912, swimming meets for women were added to the Olympic schedule.

At present, Olympic events comprise the following:

MEN—100 meter free style, 400 meter free style, 1,500 meter free style, 100 meter backstroke, 100 meter breaststroke, 200 meter breaststroke, 200 meter butterfly, 400 meter breaststroke, 800 meter free-style relay, 400 meter medley relay.

WOMEN—100 meter free style, 400 meter free style, 100 meter backstroke, 100 meter butterfly, 200 meter breaststroke, 400 meter medley relay, 400 meter free style relay.

NOTE—The medley swim is a race one-fourth of the distance of which is butterfly stroke, one-fourth backstroke, one-fourth breaststroke, one-fourth crawl stroke—in that order.

Chapter 14

WATER SAFETY

SENSIBLE precautions can do much to limit the accidents and fatalities which are an unpleasant accompaniment of the water-sports boom. Experience at Boy Scout and summer camps has indicated that the most common causes of waterfront tragedies are physical conditions such as heart diseases, epilepsy, fainting spells, and exhaustion. Failure to cling to capsized or swamped boats, and diving into shallow water, or striking underwater boulders or other obstructions, account for numerous accidents.

Water activity should be limited for individuals with a history of heart disease, epilepsy, or ear or sinus problems. Sinus and middle-ear infections are among the hazards of participation in water sports. These can be controlled if swimmers learn proper breathing from the start. Some specific safeguards are these: avoid entering the water from any height feetfirst, without holding the nose; avoid swallowing water while swimming or blowing the nose during and after swimming; avoid forceful expulsion of air while under water. Some camps observe a practice of applying a few drops of rubbing alcohol with an eye dropper to each outer ear following swimming, to aid in drying the ear passage and to prevent fungus ear infections.

Overlong immersion in water can be hazardous. Most

water activities are strenuous and lower the resistance of the individual, and water temperature is an important factor in determining the safe swimming period. The ideal temperature for swimming is considered to be 78 to 80 degrees, and while individuals differ in their tolerance to water immersion, children should be limited to no more than 30 minutes in a swimming period, and 2 swimming periods during any one day. If the water temperature is 70 degrees or below, the swimming period should be reduced accordingly.

One of the cardinal rules in boating safety is "never leave the boat in case of accident." A capsized or swamped wooden boat or canoe, or a fiberglass boat with built-in flotation, can support its passengers if they hold to the craft, keep their noses and mouths out of water, and do not try to climb aboard. If the boat is swamped topside up, the accepted practice is to put the nonswimmers or weaker swimmers inside the boat and try to "swim" it toward shore.

The bottom of any unfamiliar swimming area should be carefully examined to establish its formation and to discover any deep holes, stumps or rocks. Unless the swimming area is marked and supervised, a diving entry should never be used. It is safer to wade into the water, descend from a ladder, or use a "jump" entry. In ocean swimming, consideration should be given to undertows and the fact that offshore sand bars are highly unstable and subject to changes from tide and currents.

At the waterfront, or even in a home pool, a beginners' area should be marked off, and very young children or nonswimmers restricted to that area. This section can be marked off by using light rope or sash cord with brightly painted wooden floats. Small metal weights can serve as anchors to keep the buoy line in place. In lakes or bays, swimming areas can be marked off by buoys. These can be oilcans painted on the outside, or glass jugs painted on the inside. A jug can easily be painted by pouring some light enamel inside, replacing the cap, and shaking and turning the jug to spread the enamel while it is drying.

The Buddy System

The buddy system is in almost universal use in camps and in larger pools for group swimming. In this system every swimmer is paired with another swimmer in his own ability group. A check is made every 10 minutes and just before all swimmers leave the water. The signal for a buddy check is generally a single blast on a whistle or horn, or a bell signal. At the signal, each pair of buddies holds hands, remains silent, not moving until they receive the O.K. in the form of 2 blasts from the whistle.

During swimming, the buddies are expected to remain together, watch each other, and aid the other if he should have any difficulty.

Many skin-diving groups operate on a buddy system, and a similar setup should be arranged for any large group, or even for a family outing into the water.

Life Belts and Vests

While modern practice is to teach swimming with no artificial aids to body buoyancy, various types of life belts and vests have their place as safety factors in water sports. For a number of years, a water-skiers' life belt has been available. Fitting around the waist, it provides a measure of buoyancy and will keep the body above water. While it is small enough not to interfere with the skier's activities, it does keep the head above water if the user should become unconscious or disabled. There are also a number of different types of inflatable belts available, usually using a carbon-dioxide container which releases the gas into the belts when the release valve is opened. Also available are several types

1.

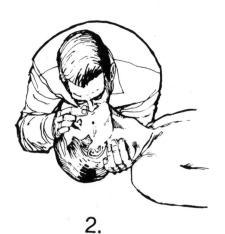

2.

HOW TO CARE FOR A PERSON WHO STOPS BREATHING

You can breathe for him and may keep him alive until medical help arrives. Many lives have been saved because someone knew how to do this. A person can stop breathing from abuse of drugs and alcohol, drowning, gas poisoning, electric shock, choking, heart failure, smothering, or other causes. The fastest and best way to get air into him is to blow air into his mouth and lungs. This is called mouth-to-mouth artificial respiration.

HOW TO DO IT

1. If you can see anything in the mouth of the person who is not breathing, turn his head to one side and clean out his mouth. Put the victim on his back. Tilt his head back so that his chin points up. Sometimes he will then start to breathe by himself.
2. If he does not start to breathe by himself when you have done this, then you will need to start blowing into his mouth. Keep his head tilted back and with one hand pinch his nose shut to keep the air from coming out there. Make an airtight seal with your mouth over the victim's mouth and then blow into his mouth until you can see his chest rise.
3. Raise your mouth after each time you blow and turn your face to the side and listen for air to come out of his lungs. Blow air into the mouth about 12 times a minute for a grown person. If you blow every 5 seconds for adults, that will be 12 times a minute. For children, use short puffs every 3 seconds. That will be about 20 times a minute. Keep this up until medical help arrives or until the person starts to breathe by himself.

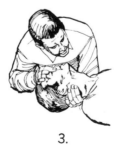

3.

of "invisible" life belts which can be worn under the trunks or bathing suit and which are inflated by opening a cartridge of gas.

However, none of the inflatable types of life preservers have the approval of the United States Coast Guard. The Coast Guard requires that all powered pleasure craft carry an approved vest-type life jacket or buoyant seat cushion for each person aboard the craft. The approved vest-type jackets have the advantage that they are designed to keep the head of the wearer above water. These are available in adult size and in several children's sizes, and their use for young children is highly recommended.

First Aid

Sunburn, cuts, bruises, sprains, possible fractures, and drowning are the waterfront or water-sports hazards. A first-aid kit should be at every waterfront location and aboard every boat. At a minimum it should contain fresh first-aid supplies, adhesive bandage, sterile gauze pads, waterproof adhesive tape, triangle bandages, sunburn lotion and a warm blanket. In case of serious injury, attempts should be made to stop any bleeding, the patient should be wrapped in the blanket, and medical aid obtained.

Every person who participates in water activities should be prepared to give artificial respiration when necessary to restore breathing. The chart on pages 230 and 231 graphically details the currently approved method of artificial respiration.

Bibliography

AMATEUR ATHLETIC UNION OF THE UNITED STATES, *Rules for Competitive and Synchronized Swimming, Diving . . . Water Polo.* 1968.

ANDERSON, LUTHER A., *A Guide to Canoe Camping.* Chicago, Reilly & Lee, 1969.

ARMBRUSTER, DAVID A., *Swimming and Diving.* 5th ed. St. Louis, Mosby, 1968.

AYMAR, GORDON CHRISTIAN, *Yacht Racing Rules and Tactics.* 6th ed. New York, Van Nostrand-Reinhold, 1970.

BATTERMAN, CHARLES, *How to Star in Swimming and Diving.* (Gr. 7-11) New York, Four Winds Press, 1970.

————, *The Techniques of Springboard Diving.* Cambridge, Mass., MIT Press, 1968.

BAVIER, ROBERT NEWTON, *The New Yacht Racing Rules.* Rev. ed. New York, Norton, 1969.

————, *Sailing to Win.* Rev. ed. New York, Dodd, 1969.

BLAIR, CLAY, *Diving for Pleasure and Treasure.* Cleveland, World Pub. Co., 1960.

BLANDFORD, PERCY W., *Canoes and Canoeing.* New York, Grosset & Dunlap, 1968.

BLOOMFIELD, JOHN, *Know-How in the Surf.* Rutland, Vt., Tuttle Co., 1965.

BOY SCOUTS OF AMERICA, *Water Skiing.* (Gr. 6-12) New Brunswick, N.J., BSA, 1969.

BROWN, ALAN, *Invitation to Sailing.* New York, Simon & Schuster, 1968.

CALAHAN, HAROLD AUGUSTIN, *Yachtsman's Omnibus.* New York, Macmillan, 1951.

CLARKE, DERRICK HARRY, *The Lure of the Sea: An Escapist Guide to Running Away to Sea in Your Own Boat.* New York, Fernhill House, 1970.

Council for National Cooperation in Aquatics, *The New Science of Skin and Scuba Diving*, 3d rev. ed. New York, Association Press, 1968.

Council for National Cooperation in Aquatics, *Water Fun for Everyone* (Gr. 9 & up) New York, Association Press, 1965.

Dixon, Conrad, *Sailing with Children*. New York, Fernhill House, 1969.

Dixon, Peter L., *The Complete Book of Surfing*. New York, Coward-McCann, 1967.

Dueker, Christopher W., *Medical Aspects of Sport Diving*. South Brunswick, N.J., A. S. Barnes, 1970.

Eaves, George, *Diving: The Mechanics of Springboard and Firmboard Techniques*. South Brunswick, N.J., A. S. Barnes, 1969.

Frey, Hank, *Camera Below: The Complete Guide to the Art and Science of Underwater Photography*. New York, Association Press, 1968.

Gabrielsen, M. A., *Aquatics Handbook*. 2d ed. Englewood Cliffs, N.J., Prentice-Hall, 1968.

Hampton, Capt. T. A., *The Master Diver and Underwater Sportsman*. Rev. ed. New York, Arco, 1970.

Hester, Ralph, *Instant Water Skiing*. New York, Grosset & Dunlap, 1965.

Howard-Williams, Jeremy, *Racing Dinghy Sails*. Chicago, Quadrangle Books, 1971.

Jarvis, Margaret Ada, *Your Book of Diving*. (Gr. 7 & up) Levittown, N.Y., Transatlantic, 1959.

———, *Your Book of Survival Swimming and Life Saving*. (Gr. 6 & up) Levittown, N.Y., Transatlantic, (n.d.).

———, *Your Book of Swimming*. (Gr. 7 & up) Levittown, N.Y., Transatlantic (n.d.).

Jones, Theodore A., *Learn to Sail*. Chicago, Rand McNally, 1971.

236

KENYON, LEY, AND HAAS, W. DE, *Aqualung Diving: A Complete and Practical Guide to the Underwater World.* London, G. Allen, 1970.

LAMBERT, ARTHUR F., *The Technique of Water Polo.* North Hollywood, Calif., Swimming World, 1969.

McALLISTER, EVELYN DITTON, *Easy Steps to Safe Swimming.* 4th rev. ed. New York, A. S. Barnes, 1970.

McDERMOTT, THOMAS JOSEPH, *Sailboat Racing Rules.* Chicago, Quadrangle Books, 1970.

McDONALD, KENDALL, *How to Get More Fun from Your Boat.* Levittown, N.Y., Transatlantic, 1970.

———,*The Underwater Book.* New Rochelle, N.Y., Sportshelf & Soccer Associates, 1969.

MALO, JOHN, *Malo's Complete Guide to Canoeing and Canoe-Camping.* Chicago, Quadrangle Books, 1969.

MERTENS, LAWRENCE EDWIN, *In-Water Photography.* New York, Interscience, 1970.

PEARSON, EVERETT A., *The Lure of Sailing.* New York, Harper, 1965.

PERRY, RONALD H., *Canoeing for Beginners.* (Gr. 9 & up) New York, Association Press, 1967.

RACKHAM, GEORGE, *Synchronized Swimming.* Levittown, N.Y., Transatlantic, 1968.

RICHARDSON, BILL, *Dinghy Racing.* New Rochelle, N.Y., Sportshelf & Soccer Associates, 1970.

RIGG, H. K., *Rigg's Handbook of Nautical Etiquette.* New York, Knopf, 1971.

RIVIERE, WILLIAM A., *Pole, Paddle & Portage.* New York, Van Nostrand-Reinhold Co., 1969.

ROBINSON, BILL, *Bill Robinson's Book of Expert Sailing.* New York, Scribner, 1965.

SHIELDS, CORNELIUS, *Cornelius Shields on Sailing.* Englewood Cliffs, N.J., Prentice-Hall, 1964.

237

SPEARS, BETTY MARY, *Fundamentals of Synchronized Swimming*. Minneapolis, Minn., Burgess Pub. Co., 1966.

STARCK, W., AND BRUNDZA, PAUL, *Art of Underwater Photography*. New York, Amphoto, 1966.

SWEENEY, JOHN, *Skin Diving and Exploring Underwater*. New York, McGraw-Hill, 1955.

TERRELL, MARK, *The Principles of Diving*. South Brunswick, N.J., A. S. Barnes, 1967.

TORNEY, JOHN A., AND CLAYTON, R. D., *Aquatic Instruction, Coaching, and Management*. South Brunswick, N.J., A. S. Barnes, 1970.

U.S. COAST GUARD, *Recreational Boating Guide*. Revised. Washington, D.C., 1966.

VICKERS, BETTY J., *Teaching Synchronized Swimming*. Englewood Cliffs, N.J., Prentice-Hall, 1965.

WHITNEY, PETER DWIGHT, *White-water Sport: Running Rapids in Kayak and Canoe*. New York, Ronald Press Co., 1960.

WILLIAMS, PETER FAIRNEY, *Canoeing Skills and Canoe Expedition Technique for Teachers and Leaders*. New Rochelle, N.Y., Sportshelf & Soccer Associates, 1967.

WILSON, PAUL C., *Modern Rowing*. Harrisburg, Pa., Stackpole Books, 1969.

YATES, FERN, AND ANDERSON, THERESA W., *Swimming*. 2d ed. New York, Ronald Press Co., 1958.

Acknowledgments

ACKNOWLEDGMENTS

For information on water skiing, the author wishes to thank the American Water Ski Association, 7th Street & Avenue G, S.W., Winter Haven, Florida; the Evinrude Foundation of Milwaukee, Wisconsin; and Cypress Gardens, Florida.

The United States Divers Co., of Santa Ana California, and Mike Burns and Bill Barada of that organization have been most helpful in providing information on skin and scuba diving. Also Florida's Silver Springs, and Jordan Klein of Underwater Sports, Miami, Florida; the Underwater Section of the Los Angeles County Department of Parks and Recreation. The United States Navy Publication *Diving Manual* has been a valuable source of technical data.

Eastman Kodak Company of Rochester, New York, has provided helpful information on underwater photography, as did the Fenjohn Company of Ardrome, Pennsylvania, and Underwater Sports, Inc.

Much information on white-water surfing was provided by the American White Water Affiliation, 5525 E. Bails Drive, Denver 22, Colorado, and by reference to its publication *American White Water,* and by Clyde Jones and Peter Whitney of that association. Valuable assistance in preparing the revised edition was provided by James C. Sindelar and Don Golden of that association.

The Hawaiian Visitors' Bureau and the Los Angeles Department of Parks and Recreation have been helpful in providing material on surfboarding.

In the section on water games, the information on double

241

water ball, and water box ball is used with permission of Nathan H. Kaufman, of Pittsburgh, Pennsylvania, columnist for *Swimming Pool Age* magazine, originator and copyrighter of the games. A number of the comedy dives are used with the permission of Rolland Hill, Director of Safety Services, Newark, New Jersey Chapter, American Red Cross. Information on competitive diving and swimming is from the *Official Swimming Guide* of the Amateur Athletic Union of the United States.

The files of *Swimming Pool Age* magazine, 425 Park Avenue S., New York City, formerly *Beach and Pool,* have been a valuable source of background information on aquatic sports and water games.

The Bibliography is largely the work of Mrs. Doris F. Borrner, Librarian, Marsh Memorial Library, Springfield, Massachusetts.

For their kind permission to reproduce the photographs in this book, the author wishes to thank the following: Evinrude Motors, Inc.; Florida Cypress Gardens Association, Inc. Mercury Outboard Motors; Australian News and Information Bureau; Scott Outboard Photos; Virgin Islands News Bureau; Florida's Silver Springs; Jordan Klein and Underwater Sports, Inc.; Hans Klepper Foldboats.

Index

Abalone, gathering, 108–9
Accessories, scuba diving, 98–102
  depth gauge, 99–100
  earplugs, 102
  flashlight, 100–1
  foot protection, 102
  goggles, 102
  knife and belt, 98
  life jacket, 98
  life lines, 101–2
  noseclip, 102
  swim fins, 98–99
  wrist compass, 100
  wristwatch, 100
Acrobat dive, 191
Air compressors, 96
Air embolism, 75
Air Lung, Northill Company, 88, 96
Air-reserve mechanism, 89
American Amateur Athletic Association, 111, 152, 193, 198, 205, 225
American Canoe Association, 163, 164
American Red Cross, 137
American Water Ski Association, 34, 36, 45
American White Water, 146
American White Water Affiliation, 146–50
Ape dive, 186
Applause dive, 187
Aqualung, the, 72–73
  United States Divers' Corporation, 88, 94–95

Aquaplane, building an, 52–53
Aquaplaning, 47–53
  development of, 50–52
Artificial respiration, 230–31, 232

Back handspring dive, 192
Backstroke, 208–9, 224–26
Ball tag, 172
Balloon race, 182
Balsa wood boards, 140
Banana peel dive, 188
Bargain basement dive, 190
Baseball, water, 217
Basketball, water, 216–17
Belts
  knife, 98
  life, 229–32
Bends, 78
Bicycle dive, 186
Blowing race, 182
Boat
  speeds, water-skiing tournament regulations, 37, 42
  water skier's, 18–19
Borelli, Giovanni, 69–70
Bourdon tube depth gauge, 100
Bournemouth Rowing Club, 201
Box ball, water, 214–15
Boxing on a raft, 189
Boy Scouts of America, 56, 62, 65, 227
Break the balloon, 218
Breaststroke, 208, 223–24
Breathing tubes, 91
Broken back jackknife dive, 189
Broken spring dive, 189